WEAVING SUNDOWN
IN A SCARLET LIGHT

❦

ALSO BY JOY HARJO

Poetry

An American Sunrise

Conflict Resolution for Holy Beings

She Had Some Horses

How We Became Human: New and Selected Poems, 1975–2001

A Map to the Next World

The Woman Who Fell from the Sky

Fishing

In Mad Love and War

Secrets from the Center of the World (with photographs by
Stephen E. Strom)

What Moon Drove Me to This?

The Last Song

Memoir

Poet Warrior

Crazy Brave

As Editor

Living Nations, Living Words: An Anthology of First Peoples Poetry

*When the Light of the World Was Subdued, Our Songs Came Through:
A Norton Anthology of Native Nations Poetry* (with LeAnne Howe,
Jennifer Elise Foerster, and contributing editors)

*Reinventing the Enemy's Language: Contemporary Native Women's
Writings of North America* (with Gloria Bird)

Interviews

Soul Talk, Song Language: Conversations with Joy Harjo (with Tanaya Winder)

The Spiral of Memory (edited by Laura Coltelli)

Music Albums

I Pray for My Enemies

Red Dreams: A Trail Beyond Tears

Winding Through the Milky Way

She Had Some Horses

Native Joy for Real

Letter from the End of the Twentieth Century

Plays

We Were There When Jazz Was Invented

Wings of Night Sky, Wings of Morning Light

Children's Books

For a Girl Becoming (illustrated by Mercedes McDonald)

The Good Luck Cat (illustrated by Paul Lee)

WEAVING
SUNDOWN
IN A
SCARLET
LIGHT

*Fifty Poems
for
Fifty Years*

JOY HARJO

W. W. NORTON & COMPANY
Celebrating a Century of Independent Publishing

For my children

Phil Dayn Wilmon Bush and Rainy Dawn Ortiz.

For then, now, and forever.

CONTENTS

❦❦❦

CONTENTS

FOREWORD

Once in a seminar class, Joy leaned over to me and whispered, "We're sitting in the back of the room. Just like Indians!" Then she dodged behind the bird wing of her hair, crinkled her nose, and laughed.

It was only then I realized something major.

I was an Indian too!

The derisive Mexican phrase "pareces indio" rose in my mind. I'd heard it often enough growing up, spoken so ubiquitously even los indios apologized for being indios. Then a more profound realization followed.

I understood why los indios kept silent.

Joy and I coincided at the University of Iowa's Writers' Workshop, where we were both enrolled in the poetry workshop from 1976 to 1978. She was a young woman in her mid-twenties who had just recently abandoned visual arts and declared herself a citizen of poetry. She had two children, at least one marriage that I knew of behind her, and was making monthly payments on a red pickup truck she had driven from New Mexico to Iowa all by herself. I didn't even have a driver's license. Joy knew how to make coffee, feed a baby from her own body, change a tire, abandon a destructive relationship, work a job, raise her kids as a single mom, drive across country with no credit cards, and write poetry after cooking and washing dishes. And she had a book. A chapbook, but an honest-to-God book. Which in my wobbly youth meant she was a real writer. I was twenty-one, but I felt like I was eleven.

She also had something I longed for. A homeland. I was still searching for mine. Joy writes: "My voice found itself, then rooted itself in the Sandia Mountains, the Rio Grande River, in the sunrises and sunsets of the Southwest.... That's when I began writing poetry, real poetry."

Joy and the kids lived in married student housing, a complex of buildings that had once been army barracks. The cinder-block walls were painted an institutional color, beige or pale green in my memory. Only Joy's beautiful Southwestern blankets saved that space from despair.

When Joy drove away one weekend for an out-of-town gig, I babysat. I remember I followed the twin lights of her truck backing out of the parking lot and listened to the wheels crunch over gravel. And I knew and felt the terror and loneliness of what it was to be a woman with two kids living in married student housing all alone during the Iowa winter.

In the beginning, I entered the workshop with the foolish bravado of my undergrad years where I had been the star writer. I remember speaking in workshop and finding an icy silence that followed. It made me think twice about ever venturing to speak again.

And for Joy, it was even worse. When we were asked to name a favorite poet, Joy claimed a feminist poet, obviously the wrong choice. There followed a winter chill—from everyone in the class including the teacher, who perhaps was not intending to be cruel, but whose silence was the cruelest of all. I want to believe that instructor was more frightened than we were; I have to believe this in order to forgive her. The discomfort I felt for Joy, the hard and deliberate silence after she spoke, this I remember too clearly.

To be truthful, other instructors after that were more welcoming, but that initial semester was devastating. I considered dropping out and going back home, and maybe I would have if Joy hadn't been there.

Joy introduced me to the Native American/Chicano Center on campus. I know I would not have sought it out myself. In public I learned keeping silent was a means to survival.

In a seminar class, Joy and I teamed up for a collaborative assignment and wrote this poem together during this season. The title says it all:

Permission to Speak

lately
i've turned to the river
to the starlings gathering there at twilight
moon in their throats

all i want is the music
anything
to keep me breathing
this dancing
this whirl of my heart

This poem was influenced by the pre-conquest Aztec poets I was reading and, of course, Joy's own poetry. Poco a poco I was becoming Indian without realizing it.

When I was floundering to find myself as a woman, a writer, it took Joy to bring me back to who I really was. She was a guide without realizing she was a guide. Her poems mapped my route home.

Just before we graduated from Iowa, Joy won a National Endowment for the Arts Fellowship. She was suddenly invited to parties by the in-crowd where once she had been ignored. It was a hypocrisy not lost on me, and I wondered if Joy felt the same.

Years later, I remember asking Joy what she had learned from that time in Iowa, and I was surprised by her answer. Grace, she said. What did she mean by that? Here in this collection, there is a poem with that title. "We had to swallow that town with laughter, so it would go down easy as honey. And one morning as the sun struggled to break ice, and our dreams had found us with coffee and pancakes in a truck stop along Highway 80, we found grace."

At Iowa I had often found myself watching Joy from afar because I didn't feel comfortable among writers who were a lifetime older than me. They played pool and smoked. They had apartments. I lived in graduate housing and ate at the same cafeteria with the football players until I couldn't stand it anymore and defected to an apartment in the basement of a little house. I watched Joy live her writer's life without knowing how difficult her days were until I read these poems.

"I did not have words . . . or anyone to speak to about what was happening. . . . Poetry gave me words to speak what had no words."

She confessed to her poetry.

In her notes about her poem "Are You Still There?" Joy writes that she "often felt voiceless." In the poem itself, the words are snagged on the barbed wire fence, shredded and silent, the phone seemingly dead. This poem illuminates her voicelessness but gives her silence a voice. It is the sound of the wind. It is haunting. It reminded me of how when I was a young woman in my twenties I kept so much inside. My conversations were running monologues in my head, not spoken aloud, only braved on paper, gingerly. I was afraid of my own poems and what they said about me. Joy was already exploring her feminist voice. Speaking it through her poems. Gathering her strength. Giving strength to others like me without knowing it.

Eventually Joy would also claim music as her country, teaching herself to play the saxophone and setting her poems to song. And even singing them aloud in front of an audience. Machu Picchu!

When she sent me her CD, and I first heard her singing voice, I was startled. It was a voice as soft as the wings of sparrows, as sweet and transparent as rain, so unlike her deeper speaking voice, a wonder to me. Where had she hidden that voice all those years? More important, why?

"I felt so far away from myself there," Joy wrote about our time together in grad school.

She clung from the thirteenth-floor window and climbed back into her life. Poetry became her own lifeline. Wondrous woman. And the poems sent lifelines to other women like me.

For a time, she lived in New Mexico and I lived in Texas, and though they are right next door to one another, we only intersected at literary events where we were both invited performers, because we didn't have money or that more expensive gift—time. Often, I was disappointed when Joy had to retreat to her room to finish something due the next day instead of having coffee with me. She had to. She was raising two kids and was obliged to work even while staying at hotels or flying on planes.

We were both married to poetry. It meant serving poetry faithfully, packing up for poetry, a husband whose career we had to follow. It meant taking the teaching gigs that came along even across the country. Taking any gig whenever/wherever we could get them. Being invited places and not having a credit card. I remember those days. How could I forget? I made it a point when I ran a literature program of paying the guest poet upon arrival so they could eat. I wish someone had thought to do the same for me and Joy.

I remember that time she walked away from a jewel of a job in the Southwest on principle. How difficult that was for her. She did so to honor a student and to protest the university's handling of the student's complaint against an instructor. She had stood her ground even if it meant resigning from a good university position, which are rare for poets to come by. I admired her integrity, her courage to live her principles, even as I grieved how hard the following years were going to be for her.

So it was that we put our heads down to work, to write, aware always that the other was creating, she with her family obligations, me wrapped up in my own warp and weft, each weaving a cloth of our own lives.

And when I raised my head, seasons had passed.

In Minneapolis we shared the live stage of the *Prairie Home Companion* radio show in a series called "Friends." I was thrilled when Joy called to invite me to be on stage with her. It wasn't the prestige of the show so much. What honored me was that I was no longer the kid sister. I had graduated to "friend."

Joy writes: "The voice of my poems is not something I had to search to find. It was there, even before I agreed to write poetry. . . . My voice is older, and I am finally growing into it."

Joy's poetry voice is indeed ancient. She has always been a visionary. A healer. A guide. She has been singing with words before she sang with notes on her sax.

The poems in this collection are gathered to serve a lifetime: births ("Rainy Dawn" and "A Map to the Next World"), deaths ("The Dawn Appears With Butterflies"), partings ("Washing My Mother's Body"), prayers ("Remember," "Eagle Poem," "This Morning I Pray for My Enemies"), blessings ("The Creation Story"), protests ("For Anna Mae Pictou Aquash"), homages ("Bird"), incantations ("Praise the Rain"), instruction ("A Postcolonial Tale" and "For Calling the Spirit Back"), songs ("Fall Song" and "How Love Blows Through the Trees"), history lessons ("New Orleans," "Tobacco Origin Story," and "Rabbit Is Up To Tricks"), medicine ("I Give You Back"), resistance ("No").

Joy has written in secret, in silence, been an apprentice when I met her and evolved into a word worker, a teacher, a healer, a navigator to illuminate us in our journey. She holds memory. Listens with more than her heart. In this capacity she is a translator. The woman priestess Joy was always una diosa to me, una shamana, a seer.

I keep her words within reach on my bedside to give me strength, to give me clarity, especially during these difficult political times. When I read her poetry, I am inspired to answer and write poetry. How many times have I read "I Give You Back" to myself, to others?

Once she was the quiet girl. Now she sings for a nation. Her voice is strong. She speaks for those afraid to speak their histories, as in her Tulsa poem "Somewhere."

Singer of songs, storyteller, memory keeper, teacher, interpreter of ghosts, of the stars, of the ancestors. Respected elder. Wise woman. Channeler.

The poems in this collection are a song cycle, a woman warrior's journey in this era, reaching backward and forward and waking in the present moment. A chant for survival.

Joy speaks American history, episodes not part of the official story. Speaks bravely about the atrocities. Finds a way into the abandoned story and opens the doors and windows. She has found the power to make change by retelling the story.

Then came the news. I was as surprised as Joy to learn she had become the national poet laureate. We had to laugh. I wrote, "No one could invent our destinies."

I've only known Joy forty-six of the fifty years documented in these pages. I watched her early on attempting flight, a young woman just discovering poetry. I watched her when she first began to soar and wheel into the ether. And sometimes I lost sight of her for several years when she flew above the horizon until she came back into the scope of my vision, appearing out of dawn, descending briefly into my life, and gracefully alighting.

We are all a cloth woven into existence, extending out and connecting to everyone and everything. A weaving I have witnessed from early on when it was only early morning. Now here we are nearing sundown, walking "to the edge of the story. . . ." The weave of our life cloth has not intersected as often as I would like, but the design is beautiful just as it is.

In these poems I hear Joy singing, "Pass this love on."

Sandra Cisneros
February 21, 2022
Casa Coatlicue
San Miguel de Allende

WEAVING SUNDOWN
IN A SCARLET LIGHT

THE LAST SONG

how can you stand it
he said
the hot oklahoma summers
where you were born
this humid thick air
is choking me
and i want to go back
to new mexico

it is the only way
i know how to breathe
an ancient chant
that my mother knew
came out of a history
woven from wet tall grass
in her womb
and i know no other way
than to surround my voice
with the summer songs of crickets
in this moist south night air

oklahoma will be the last song
i'll ever sing

ARE YOU STILL THERE?

there are sixty-five miles
of telephone wire
between acoma
    and albuquerque
i dial the number
and listen for the sound
of his low voice
    on the other side
hello
  is a gentle motion of a western wind
cradling tiny purple flowers
that grow near the road
      towards laguna
i smell them
as i near the rio puerco bridge
my voice stumbles
returning over sandstone
    as it passes the cañoncito exit
i have missed you he says
the rhythm circles the curve
of mesita cliffs
    to meet me
but my voice is caught
shredded on a barbed wire fence
at the side of the road
and flutters soundless
in the wind

ANCHORAGE

for Audre Lorde

This city is made of stone, of blood, and fish.
There are Chugach Mountains to the east
and whale and seal to the west.
It hasn't always been this way, because glaciers
who are ice ghosts create oceans, carve earth
and shape this city here, by the sound.
They swim backwards in time.

Once a storm of boiling earth cracked open
the streets, threw open the town.
It's quiet now, but underneath the concrete
is the cooking earth,
          and above that, air
which is another ocean, where spirits we can't see
are dancing   joking   getting full
on roasted caribou, and the praying
goes on, extends out.

Nora and I go walking down Fourth Avenue
and know it is all happening.
On a park bench we see someone's Athabascan
grandmother, folded up, smelling like 200 years
of blood and piss, her eyes closed against some
unimagined darkness, where she is buried
in an ache in which nothing makes sense.

We keep on breathing, walking, but softer now,
the clouds whirling in the air above us.
What can we say that would make us understand
better than we do already?
Except to speak of her home and claim her
as our own history, and know that our dreams
don't end here, two blocks away from the ocean
where our hearts still batter away at the muddy shore.

And I think of the Sixth Avenue jail, of mostly Native
and Black men, where Henry told about being shot at
eight times outside a liquor store in L.A., but when
the car sped away he was surprised he was alive,
no bullet holes, man, and eight cartridges strewn
on the sidewalk all around him.

Everyone laughed at the impossibility of it,
but also the truth. Because who would believe
the fantastic and terrible story of all of our survival
those who were never meant

                              to survive?

FOR ALVA BENSON, AND FOR THOSE WHO HAVE LEARNED TO SPEAK

And the ground spoke when she was born.
Her mother heard it. In Navajo she answered
as she squatted down against the earth
to give birth. It was now when it happened,
now giving birth to itself again and again
between the legs of women.

Or maybe it was the Indian Hospital
in Gallup. The ground still spoke beneath
mortar and concrete. She strained against the
metal stirrups, and they tied her hands down
because she still spoke with them when they
muffled her screams. But her body went on
talking and the child was born into their
hands, and the child learned to speak
both voices.

She grew up talking in Navajo, in English
and watched the earth around her shift and change
with the people in the towns and in the cities
learning not to hear the ground as it spun around
beneath them. She learned to speak for the ground,
the voice coming through her like roots that
have long hungered for water. Her own daughter
was born, like she had been, in either place
or all places, so she could leave, leap
into the sound she had always heard,

a voice like water, like the gods weaving
against sundown in a scarlet light.

The child now hears names in her sleep.
They change into other names, and into others.
It is the ground murmuring, and Mount St. Helens
erupts as the harmonic motion of a child turning
inside her mother's belly waiting to be born
to begin another time.

And we go on, keep giving birth and watch
ourselves die, over and over.
And the ground spinning beneath us
goes on talking.

THE WOMAN HANGING FROM THE
THIRTEENTH-FLOOR WINDOW

She is the woman hanging from the 13th-floor
window. Her hands are pressed white against the
concrete molding of the tenement building. She
hangs from the 13th-floor window in east Chicago,
with a swirl of birds over her head. They could
be a halo, or a storm of glass waiting to crush her.

She thinks she will be set free.

The woman hanging from the 13th-floor window
on the east side of Chicago is not alone.
She is a woman of children, of the baby, Carlos,
and of Margaret, and of Jimmy who is the oldest.
She is her mother's daughter and her father's son.
She is several pieces between the two husbands
she has had. She is all the women of the apartment
building who stand watching her, watching themselves.

When she was young she ate wild rice on scraped-down
plates in warm wood rooms. It was in the farther
north and she was the baby then. They rocked her.

She sees Lake Michigan lapping at the shores of
herself. It is a dizzy hole of water and the rich
live in tall glass houses at the edge of it. In some
places Lake Michigan speaks softly, here, it just sputters
and butts itself against the asphalt. She sees
other buildings just like hers. She sees other

women hanging from many-floored windows
counting their lives in the palms of their hands
and in the palms of their children's hands.

She is the woman hanging from the 13th-floor window
on the Indian side of town. Her belly is soft from
her children's births, her worn Levi's swing down below
her waist, and then her feet, and then her heart.
She is dangling.

The woman hanging from the 13th floor hears voices.
They come to her in the night when the lights have gone
dim. Sometimes they are little cats mewing and scratching
at the door, sometimes they are her grandmother's voice,
and sometimes they are gigantic men of light whispering
to her to get up, to get up, get up. That's when she wants
to have another child to hold on to in the night, to be able
to fall back into dreams.

And the woman hanging from the 13th-floor window
hears other voices. Some of them scream out from below
for her to jump, they would push her over. Others cry softly
from the sidewalks, pull their children up like flowers and gather
them into their arms. They would help her, like themselves.

But she is the woman hanging from the 13th-floor window,
and she knows she is hanging by her own fingers, her
own skin, her own thread of indecision.

She thinks of Carlos, of Margaret, of Jimmy.
She thinks of her father, and of her mother.
She thinks of all the women she has been, of all
the men. She thinks of the color of her skin, and
of Chicago streets, and of waterfalls and pines.
She thinks of moonlight nights, and of cool spring storms.
Her mind chatters like neon and northside bars.
She thinks of the 4 a.m. lonelinesses that have folded
her up like death, discordant, without logical and
beautiful conclusion. Her teeth break off at the edges.
She would speak.

The woman hangs from the 13th floor crying for
the lost beauty of her own life. She sees the
sun falling west over the gray plane of Chicago.
She thinks she remembers listening to her own life
break loose, as she falls from the 13th-floor
window on the east side of Chicago, or as she
climbs back up to claim herself again.

REMEMBER

Remember the sky you were born under,
know each of the star's stories.
Remember the moon, know who she is.
Remember the sun's birth at dawn, that is the
strongest point of time. Remember sundown
and the giving away to night.
Remember your birth, how your mother struggled
to give you form and breath. You are evidence of
her life, and her mother's, and hers.
Remember your father. He is your life, also.
Remember the earth whose skin you are:
red earth, black earth, yellow earth, white earth
brown earth, we are earth.
Remember the plants, trees, animal life who all have their
tribes, their families, their histories, too. Talk to them,
listen to them. They are alive poems.
Remember the wind. Remember her voice. She knows the
origin of this universe.
Remember you are all people and all people
are you.
Remember you are this universe and this
universe is you.
Remember all is in motion, is growing, is you.
Remember language comes from this.
Remember the dance language is, that life is.
Remember.

NEW ORLEANS

This is the south. I look for evidence
of other Creeks, for remnants of voices,
or for tobacco brown bones to come wandering
down Conti Street, Royal, or Decatur.
Near the French Market I see a blue horse
caught frozen in stone in the middle of
a square. Brought in by the Spanish on
an endless ocean voyage he became mad
and crazy. They caught him in blue
rock, said

>   don't talk.

I know it wasn't just a horse

>   that went crazy.

Nearby is a shop with ivory and knives.
There are red rocks. The man behind the
counter has no idea that he is inside
magic stones. He should find out before
they destroy him. These things
have memory,

>   you know.

I have a memory.

>   It swims deep in blood,
a delta in the skin. It swims out of Oklahoma,
deep the Mississippi River. It carries my
feet to these places: the French Quarter,
stale rooms, the sun behind thick and moist

clouds, and I hear boats hauling themselves up
and down the river.

My spirit comes here to drink.
My spirit comes here to drink.
Blood is the undercurrent.

There are voices buried in the Mississippi mud.
There are ancestors and future children
buried beneath the currents stirred up by
pleasure boats going up and down.
There are stories here made of memory.

I remember De Soto. He is buried somewhere in
this river, his bones sunk like the golden
treasure he traveled half the earth to find,
came looking for gold cities, for shining streets
of beaten gold to dance on with silk ladies.

He should have stayed home.

> (Creeks knew of him for miles
> before he came into town.
> Dreamed of silver blades
> and crosses.)

And knew he was one of the ones who yearned
for something his heart wasn't big enough
to handle.
> (And De Soto thought it was gold.)

The Creeks lived in earth towns,
                    not gold,
              spun children, not gold.
That's not what De Soto thought he wanted to see.
The Creeks knew it, and drowned him in
              the Mississippi River
                         so he wouldn't have to drown himself.

Maybe his body is what I am looking for
as evidence. To know in another way
that my memory is alive.
But he must have got away, somehow,
because I have seen New Orleans,
the lace and silk buildings,
trolley cars on beaten silver paths,
graves that rise up out of soft earth in the rain,
shops that sell black mammy dolls
holding white babies.

And I know I have seen De Soto,
                    having a drink on Bourbon Street,
                    mad and crazy
                    dancing with a woman as gold
                    as the river bottom.

SHE HAD SOME HORSES

She had some horses.

She had horses who were bodies of sand.
She had horses who were maps drawn of blood.
She had horses who were skins of ocean water.
She had horses who were the blue air of sky.
She had horses who were fur and teeth.
She had horses who were clay and would break.
She had horses who were splintered red cliff.

She had some horses.

She had horses with eyes of trains.
She had horses with full, brown thighs.
She had horses who laughed too much.
She had horses who threw rocks at glass houses.
She had horses who licked razor blades.

She had some horses.

She had horses who danced in their mothers' arms.
She had horses who thought they were the sun and their
bodies shone and burned like stars.
She had horses who waltzed nightly on the moon.
She had horses who were much too shy, and kept quiet
in stalls of their own making.

She had some horses.

She had horses who liked Creek Stomp Dance songs.
She had horses who cried in their beer.
She had horses who spit at male queens who made
them afraid of themselves.
She had horses who said they weren't afraid.
She had horses who lied.
She had horses who told the truth, who were stripped
bare of their tongues.

She had some horses.

She had horses who called themselves, "horse."
She had horses who called themselves, "spirit," and kept
their voices secret and to themselves.
She had horses who had no names.
She had horses who had books of names.

She had some horses.

She had horses who whispered in the dark, who were afraid to speak.
She had horses who screamed out of fear of the silence, who
carried knives to protect themselves from ghosts.
She had horses who waited for destruction.
She had horses who waited for resurrection.

She had some horses.

She had horses who got down on their knees for any savior.
She had horses who thought their high price had saved them.
She had horses who tried to save her, who climbed in her
bed at night and prayed.

She had some horses.

She had some horses she loved.
She had some horses she hated.

These were the same horses.

I GIVE YOU BACK

I release you, my beautiful and terrible
fear. I release you. You were my beloved
and hated twin, but now, I don't know you
as myself. I release you with all the
pain I would know at the death of
my children.

You are not my blood anymore.

I give you back to the soldiers
who burned down my home, beheaded my children,
raped and sodomized my brothers and sisters.
I give you back to those who stole the
food from our plates when we were starving.

I release you, fear, because you hold
these scenes in front of me and I was born
with eyes that can never close.

I release you
I release you
I release you
I release you

I am not afraid to be angry.
I am not afraid to rejoice.
I am not afraid to be black.
I am not afraid to be white.
I am not afraid to be hungry.

I am not afraid to be full.
I am not afraid to be hated.
I am not afraid to be loved.

to be loved, to be loved, fear.

Oh, you have choked me, but I gave you the leash.
You have gutted me but I gave you the knife.
You have devoured me, but I laid myself across the fire.

I take myself back, fear.
You are not my shadow any longer.
I won't hold you in my hands.
You can't live in my eyes, my ears, my voice
my belly, or in my heart my heart
my heart my heart

But come here, fear
I am alive and you are so afraid

of dying.

MY HOUSE IS THE RED EARTH

My house is the red earth; it could be the center of the world. I've heard New York, Paris, or Tokyo called the center of the world, but I say it is magnificently humble. You could drive by and miss it. Radio waves can obscure it. Words cannot construct it, for there are some sounds left to sacred wordless form. For instance, that fool crow, picking through trash near the corral, understands the center of the world as greasy scraps of fat. Just ask him. He doesn't have to say that the earth has turned scarlet through fierce belief, after centuries of heartbreak and laughter—he perches on the blue bowl of the sky, and laughs.

❘◈❘◈❘◈❘

If you look with the mind of the swirling earth near Shiprock you become the land, beautiful. And understand how three crows at the edge of the highway, laughing, become three crows at the edge of the world, laughing.

❘◈❘◈❘◈❘

Don't bother the earth spirit who lives here. She is working on a story. It is the oldest story in the world and it is delicate, changing. If she sees you watching she will invite you in for coffee, give you warm bread, and you will be obligated to stay and listen. But this is no ordinary story. You will have to endure earthquakes, lightning, the deaths of all those you love, the most blinding beauty. It's a story so compelling you may never want to leave; this is how she traps you. See that stone finger over there? That is the only one who ever escaped.

GRACE

I think of Wind and her wild ways the year we had nothing to lose and lost it anyway in the cursed country of the fox. We still talk about that winter, how the cold froze imaginary buffalo on the stuffed horizon of snowbanks. The haunting voices of the starved and mutilated broke fences, crashed our thermostat dreams, and we couldn't stand it one more time. So once again we lost a winter in stubborn memory, walked through cheap apartment walls, skated through fields of ghosts into a town that never wanted us, in the epic search for grace.

Like Coyote, like Rabbit, we could not contain our terror and clowned our way through a season of false midnights. We had to swallow that town with laughter, so it would go down easy as honey. And one morning as the sun struggled to break ice, and our dreams had found us with coffee and pancakes in a truck stop along Highway 80, we found grace.

I could say grace was a woman with time on her hands, or a white buffalo escaped from memory. But in that dingy light it was a promise of balance. We once again understood the talk of animals, and spring was lean and hungry with the hope of children and corn.

I would like to say, with grace, we picked ourselves up and walked into the spring thaw. We didn't; the next season was worse. You went home to Leech Lake to work with the tribe and I went south. And, Wind, I am still crazy. I know there is something larger than the memory of a dispossessed people. We have seen it.

DEER DANCER

Nearly everyone had left that bar in the middle of winter except the hard-core. It was the coldest night of the year, every place shut down, but not us. Of course we noticed when she came in. We were Indian ruins. She was the end of beauty. No one knew her, the stranger whose tribe we recognized, her family related to deer, if that's who she was, a people accustomed to hearing songs in pine trees, and making them hearts.

The woman inside the woman who was to dance naked in the bar of misfits blew deer magic. Henry Jack, who could not survive a sober day, thought she was Buffalo Calf Woman come back, passed out, his head by the toilet. All night he dreamed a dream he could not say. The next day he borrowed money, went home, and sent back the money I lent. Now that's a miracle. Some people see vision in a burned tortilla, some in the face of a woman.

This is the bar of broken survivors, the club of shotgun, knife wound, of poison by culture. We who were taught not to stare drank our beer. The players gossiped down their cues. Someone put a quarter in the jukebox to relive despair. Richard's wife dove to kill her. We had to hold her back, empty her pockets of knives and diaper pins, buy her two beers to keep her still, while Richard secretly bought the beauty a drink.

How do I say it? In this language there are no words for how the real world collapses. I could say it in my own and the sacred mounds would come into focus, but I couldn't take it in this dingy envelope. So I look at the stars in this strange city, frozen to the back of the sky, the only promises that ever make sense.

My brother-in-law hung out with white people, went to law school with a perfect record, quit. Says you can keep your laws, your words. And practiced law on the street with his hands. He jimmied to the proverbial dream girl, the face of the moon, while the players racked a new game. He bragged to us, he told her magic words and that's when she broke, became human.

But we all heard his bar voice crack:

What's a girl like you doing in a place like this?

That's what I'd like to know, what are we all doing in a place like this?

You would know she could hear only what she wanted to; don't we all? Left the drink of betrayal Richard bought her, at the bar. What was she on? We all wanted some. Put a quarter in the juke. We all take risks stepping into thin air. Our ceremonies didn't predict this. Or we expected more.

I had to tell you this, for the baby inside the girl sealed up with a lick of hope and swimming into praise of nations. This is not a rooming house, but a dream of winter falls and the deer who portrayed the relatives of strangers. The way back is deer breath on icy windows.

The next dance none of us predicted. She borrowed a chair for the stairway to heaven and stood on a table of names. And danced in the room of children without shoes.

You picked a fine time to leave me, Lucille.
With four hungry children and a crop in the field.

And then she took off her clothes. She shook loose memory, waltzed with the empty lover we'd all become.

She was the myth slipped down through dreamtime. The promise of feast we all knew was coming. The deer who crossed through knots of a curse to find us. She was no slouch, and neither were we, watching.

The music ended. And so does the story. I wasn't there. But I imagined her like this, not a stained red dress with tape on her heels but the deer who entered our dream in white dawn, breathed mist into pine trees, her fawn a blessing of meat, the ancestors who never left.

FOR ANNA MAE PICTOU AQUASH, WHOSE SPIRIT IS PRESENT HERE AND IN THE DAPPLED STARS (FOR WE REMEMBER THE STORY AND MUST TELL IT AGAIN SO WE MAY ALL LIVE)

Beneath a sky blurred with mist and wind,

                                        I am amazed as I watch the violet
heads of crocuses erupt from the stiff earth

                                after dying for a season,
as I have watched my own dark head

                            appear each morning after entering
the next world

                    to come back to this one,

                                    amazed.
It is the way in the natural world to understand the place

                                        the ghost dancers named
after the heart/breaking destruction.

                        Anna Mae,

                                    everything and nothing changes.
You are the shimmering young woman

                                who found her voice,
when you were warned to be silent, or have your body cut away
from you like an elegant weed.

                    You are the one whose spirit is present in the dappled stars.
(They prance and lope like colored horses who stay with us
        through the streets of these steely cities. And I have seen them
                    nuzzling the frozen bodies of tattered drunks
                    on the corner.)
This morning when the last star is dimming

                                    and the buses grind toward
the middle of the city, I know it is ten years since they buried you

the second time in Lakota, a language that could

                                       free you.

I heard about it in Oklahoma, or New Mexico,
how the wind howled and pulled everything down
in a righteous anger.
              (It was the women who told me) and we understood wordlessly
the ripe meaning of your murder.
        As I understand ten years later after the slow changing
                of the seasons
that we have just begun to touch
        the dazzling whirlwind of our anger,
we have just begun to perceive the amazed world the ghost dancers
        entered
                crazily, beautifully.

BIRD

The moon plays horn, leaning on the shoulder of the dark universe
to the infinite glitter of chance. Tonight I watched Bird kill himself,

larger than real life. I've always had a theory that some of us
are born with nerve endings longer than our bodies. Out to here,

farther than his convoluted scales could reach. Those nights he
played did he climb the stairway of forgetfulness, with his horn,

a woman who is always beautiful to strangers? All poets
understand the final uselessness of words. We are chords to

other chords to other chords, if we're lucky, to melody. The moon
is brighter than anything I can see when I come out of the theater,

than music, than memory of music, or any mere poem. At least
I can dance to "Ornithology" or sweet-talk beside "Charlie's Blues,"

but inside this poem I can't play a horn, hijack a plane to
somewhere where music is the place those nerve endings dangle.

Each rhapsody embodies counterpoint, and pain stuns the woman
in high heels, the man behind the horn, sings the heart.

To survive is sometimes a leap into madness. The fingers of
saints are still hot from miracles, but can they save themselves?

Where is the dimension a god lives who will take Bird home?
I want to see it, I said to the Catalinas, to the Rincons,

to anyone listening in the dark. I said, Let me hear you
by any means: by horn, by fever, by night, even by some poem

attempting flight home.

RAINY DAWN

I can still close my eyes and open them four floors up looking south and west from the hospital, the approximate direction of Acoma, and farther on to the roofs of the houses of the gods who have learned there are no endings, only beginnings. That day so hot, heat danced in waves off bright car tops, we both stood poised at that door from the east, listened for a long time to the sound of our grandmothers' voices, the brushing wind of sacred wings, the rattle of raindrops in dry gourds. I had to participate in the dreaming of you into memory, cupped your head in the bowl of my body as ancestors lined up to give you a name made of their dreams cast once more into this stew of precious spirit and flesh. And let you go, as I am letting you go once more in this ceremony of the living. And when you were born, I held you wet and unfolding, like a butterfly newly born from the chrysalis of my body. And breathed with you as you breathed your first breath. Then was your promise to take it on like the rest of us, this immense journey, for love, for rain.

SANTA FE

The wind blows lilacs out of the east. And it isn't lilac season. And
I am walking the street in front of St. Francis Cathedral in Santa
Fe. Oh, and it's a few years earlier and more. That's how you tell real
time. It is here, it is there. The lilacs have taken over everything: the
sky, the narrow streets, my shoulders, my lips. I talk lilac. And there
is nothing else until a woman the size of a fox breaks through the
bushes, breaks the purple web. She is tall and black and gorgeous.
She is the size of a fox on the arm of a white man who looks and
tastes like cocaine. She lies for cocaine, dangles on the arm of
cocaine. And lies to me now from a room in the DeVargas Hotel,
where she has eaten her lover, white powder on her lips. That is true
now; it is not true anymore. Eventually space curves, walks over and
taps me on the shoulder. On the sidewalk I stand near St. Francis;
he has been bronzed, a perpetual tan, with birds on his hand, his
shoulder, deer at his feet. I am Indian and in this town I will never
be a saint. I am seventeen and shy and wild. I have been up until
three at a party, but there is no woman in the DeVargas Hotel, for
that story hasn't yet been invented. A man whose face I will never
remember, and never did, drives up on a Harley-Davidson. There
are lilacs on his arm; they spill out from the spokes of his wheels.
He wants me on his arm, on the back of his lilac bike touring the
flower kingdom of San Francisco. And for a piece of time the size of
a nickel, I think, maybe. But maybe is vapor, has no anchor here in
the sun beneath St. Francis Cathedral. And space is as solid as the
bronze statue of St. Francis, the fox breaking through the lilacs, my
invention of this story, the wind blowing.

EAGLE POEM

To pray you open your whole self
To sky, to earth, to sun, to moon
To one whole voice that is you.
And know there is more
That you can't see, can't hear,
Can't know except in moments
Steadily growing, and in languages
That aren't always sound but other
Circles of motion.
Like eagle that Sunday morning
Over Salt River. Circled in blue sky
In wind, swept our hearts clean
With sacred wings.
We see you, see ourselves and know
That we must take the utmost care
And kindness in all things.
Breathe in, knowing we are made of
All this, and breathe, knowing
We are truly blessed because we
Were born, and die soon within a
True circle of motion,
Like eagle rounding out the morning
Inside us.
We pray that it will be done
In beauty.
In beauty.

THE CREATION STORY

I'm not afraid of love
or its consequence of light.

It's not easy to say this
or anything when my entrails
dangle between paradise
and fear.

I am ashamed
I never had the words
to carry a friend from her death
to the stars
correctly.

Or the words to keep
my people safe
from drought
or gunshot.

The stars who were created by words
are circling over this house
formed of calcium, of blood

this house
in danger of being torn apart
by stones of fear.

If these words can do anything
if these songs can do anything
I say bless this house
with stars.

Transfix us with love.

A POSTCOLONIAL TALE

Every day is a reenactment of the creation story. We emerge from dense unspeakable material, through the shimmering power of dreaming stuff.

This is the first world, and the last.

Once we abandoned ourselves for television, the box that separates the dreamer from the dreaming. It was as if we were stolen, put into a bag carried on the back of a man who pretends to own the earth and the sky. In the sack were all the people of the world. We fought until there was a hole in the bag.

When we fell we were not aware of falling. We were driving to work, or to the mall. The children were in school learning subtraction with guns.

We found ourselves somewhere near the diminishing point of civilization, not far from the trickster's bag of tricks. Everything was as we imagined it. The earth and stars, every creature and leaf imagined with us.

When we fell we were not aware of falling. We were driving to work or to the mall. The children were in school learning subtraction with guns.

The imagining needs praise as does any living thing.
We are evidence of this praise.
And when we laugh, we're indestructible.
No story or song will translate

the full impact of falling,
or the inverse power of rising up.
Of rising up.

Our children put down their guns when we did to imagine with us.
We imagined the shining link between the heart and the sun.
We imagined tables of food for everyone.
We imagined the songs.

The imagination conversely illumines us, speaks with us, sings with
us, drums with us, loves us.

THE DAWN APPEARS WITH BUTTERFLIES

You leave before daybreak to prepare your husband's body for
burial at dawn. It is one of countless dawns since the first crack of
consciousness, each buried in molecular memory, each as distinct as
your face in the stew of human faces, your eyes blinking back force
in the vortex of loss and heartbreak.

I put on another pot of coffee, watch out the kitchen window
at the beginning of the world, follow your difficult journey to
Flagstaff, through rocks that recall the scarlet promises of gods,
their interminable journeys, and pine. Until I can no longer see, but
continue to believe in the sun's promise to return:

And it will this morning. And tomorrow. And the day after
tomorrow, building the spiral called eternity out of each sun, the
dance of butterflies evoking the emerging.

Two nights ago you drove north from the hospital at Flagstaff, after
his abandonment to the grace we pursue as wild horses the wind.
Your grief was the dark outlining the stars. One star in particular
waved to you as you maneuvered in the nightmare of the myth
of death. It broke loose, stammered, then flew marking the place
between the star house of the gods and Third Mesa.

You laughed with the spirit of your husband who would toss stars!
And your tears made a pale butterfly, the color of dawn, which is the
color of the sky of the next world, which isn't that far away.

There is no tear in the pattern. It is perfect, as our gradual return to the maker of butterflies, or our laughter as we considered the joke of burying him in the shirt you always wanted him to wear, a shirt he hated.

Someone is singing in the village. And the sacredness of all previous dawns resonates. That is the power of the singer who respects the power of the place without words, which is as butterflies, returning to the sun, our star in the scheme of stars, of revolving worlds.

And within that the power of the dying is to know when to make that perfect leap into everything. We are all dying together, though there is nothing like the loneliness of being the first or the last, and we all take that place with each other.

In the west at every twilight since the beginning, the oldest spirits camp out with their dogs. It is always in the season just before winter. It is always shooting star weather and they wash dishes by dipping them in river water warmed in a bucket.

Coffee heats over the fire. Crows take their sacred place. The sun always returns and butterflies are a memory of one loved like no other. All events in the universe are ordinary. Even miracles occur ordinarily as spirits travel to the moon, visit distant relatives, as always.

Then at dusk they share the fire that warms the world, and sit together remembering everything, recounting the matrix of allies and enemies, of sons and daughters, of lovers and lovers, each molecule of the sky and earth an explosion of memory within us.

In this fierce drama of everything we are at this juncture of our
linked journey to the Milky Way—as your babies stir in bittersweet
dreams while you travel to your most difficult good-bye—as
Grandma lies down with them to comfort them—as your father's
truck starts down the road in the village—as a dog barks—

everything is a prayer for this journey.
As you shut the door behind you in the dark:
Wings of dusk
Wings of night sky
Wings of dawn
Wings of morning light

It is sunrise now.

PERHAPS THE WORLD ENDS HERE

The world begins at a kitchen table. No matter what, we must eat to live.

The gifts of earth are brought and prepared, set on the table. So it has been since creation, and it will go on.

We chase chickens or dogs away from it. Babies teethe at the corners. They scrape their knees under it.

It is here that children are given instructions on what it means to be human. We make men at it, we make women.

At this table we gossip, recall enemies and the ghosts of lovers.

Our dreams drink coffee with us as they put their arms around our children. They laugh with us at our poor falling-down selves and as we put ourselves back together once again at the table.

This table has been a house in the rain, an umbrella in the sun.

Wars have begun and ended at this table. It is a place to hide in the shadow of terror. A place to celebrate the terrible victory.

We have given birth on this table, and have prepared our parents for burial here.

At this table we sing with joy, with sorrow. We pray of suffering and remorse. We give thanks.

Perhaps the world will end at the kitchen table, while we are laughing and crying, eating of the last sweet bite.

A MAP TO THE NEXT WORLD

(for Desiray Kierra Chee)

In the last days of the fourth world I wished to make a map for
those who would climb through the hole in the sky.

My only tools were the desires of humans as they emerged from the
killing fields, from the bedrooms and the kitchens.

For the soul is a wanderer with many hands and feet.

The map must be of sand and can't be read by ordinary light. It must
carry fire to the next tribal town, for renewal of spirit.

In the legend are instructions on the language of the land, how it
was we forgot to acknowledge the gift, as if we were not in it or of it.

Take note of the proliferation of supermarkets and malls, the altars
of money. They best describe the detour from grace.

Keep track of the errors of our forgetfulness; the fog steals our
children while we sleep.

Flowers of rage spring up in the depression. Monsters are born there
of nuclear anger.

Trees of ashes wave good-bye to good-bye and the map appears to
disappear.

We no longer know the names of the birds here, how to speak to them by their personal names.

Once we knew everything in this lush promise.

What I am telling you is real and is printed in a warning on the map. Our forgetfulness stalks us, walks the earth behind us, leaving a trail of paper diapers, needles and wasted blood.

An imperfect map will have to do, little one.

The place of entry is the sea of your mother's blood, your father's small death as he longs to know himself in another.

There is no exit.

The map can be interpreted through the wall of the intestine—a spiral on the road of knowledge.

You will travel through the membrane of death, smell cooking from the encampment where our relatives make a feast of fresh deer meat and corn soup, in the Milky Way.

They have never left us; we abandoned them for science.

And when you take your next breath as we enter the fifth world there will be no X, no guidebook with words you can carry.

You will have to navigate by your mother's voice, renew the song she is singing.

Fresh courage glimmers from planets.

And lights the map printed with the blood of history, a map you will have to know by your intention, by the language of suns.

When you emerge note the tracks of the monster slayers where they entered the cities of artificial light and killed what was killing us.

You will see red cliffs. They are the heart, contain the ladder.

A white deer will come to greet you when the last human climbs from the destruction.

Remember the hole of shame marking the act of abandoning our tribal grounds.

We were never perfect.

Yet, the journey we make together is perfect on this earth who was once a star and made the same mistakes as humans.

We might make them again, she said.

Crucial to finding the way is this: there is no beginning or end.

You must make your own map.

EMERGENCE

It's midsummer night. The light is skinny;
a thin skirt of desire skims the earth.
Dogs bark at the musk of other dogs
and the urge to go wild.
I am lingering at the edge
of a broken heart, striking relentlessly
against the flint of hard will.
It's coming apart.
And everyone knows it.
So do squash erupting in flowers
the color of the sun.
So does the momentum of grace
gathering allies
in the partying mob.
The heart knows everything.
I remember when there was no urge
to cut the land or each other into pieces,
when we knew how to think
in beautiful.
There is no world like the one surfacing.
I can smell it as I pace in my square room,
the neighbor's television
entering my house by waves of sound
makes me think about buying
a new car, another kind of cigarette
when I don't need another car
and I don't smoke cigarettes.
A human mind is small when thinking
of small things.

It is large when embracing the maker
of walking, thinking and flying.
If I can locate the sense beyond desire,
I will not eat or drink
until I stagger into the earth
with grief.
I will locate the point of dawning
and awaken
with the longest day in the world.

THE PATH TO THE MILKY WAY LEADS THROUGH LOS ANGELES

There are strangers above me, below me, and all around me and we are all strange in this place of recent invention.

This city named for angels appears naked and stripped of anything resembling the shaking of turtle shells, the songs of human voices on a summer night outside Okmulgee.

Yet, it's perpetually summer here, and beautiful. The shimmer of gods is easier to perceive at sunrise or dusk,

when those who remember us here in the illusion of the marketplace turn toward the changing of the sun and say our names.

We matter to somebody. We must matter to the strange god who imagines us as we revolve together in the dark sky on the path to the Milky Way.

We can't easily see that starry road from the perspective of the crossing of boulevards, can't hear it in the whine of civilization or taste the minerals of planets in hamburgers.

But we can buy a map here of the stars' homes, dial a tone for dangerous love, choose from several brands of water or a hiss of oxygen for gentle rejuvenation.

Everyone knows you can't buy love but you can still sell your soul for less than a song to a stranger who will sell it to someone else for a profit until you're owned by a company of strangers in the city of the strange and getting stranger.

I'd rather understand how to sing from a crow who was never good at singing or much of anything but finding gold in the trash of humans.

So what are we doing here? I ask the crow parading on the ledge of falling that hangs over this precarious city.

Crow just laughs and says *wait, wait and see* and I am waiting and not seeing anything, not just yet.

But like crow I collect the shine of anything beautiful I can find.

EQUINOX

I must keep from breaking into the story by force,
If I do, I will find a war club in my hand
And the smoke of grief staggering toward the sun,
Your nation dead beside you.

I keep walking away though it has been an eternity
And from each drop of blood
Spring up sons and daughters, trees
A mountain of sorrows, of songs.

I tell you this from the dusk of a small city in the north
Not far from the birthplace of cars and industry.
Geese are returning to mate and crocuses have
Broken through the frozen earth.

Soon they will come for me and I will make my stand
Before the jury of destiny. Yes, I will answer in the clatter
Of the new world, I have broken my addiction to war
And desire.

I have buried the dead, and made songs of the blood,
The marrow.

There is a small mist at the brow of the mountain,

each leaf of flower, of taro, tree and bush shivers with ecstasy.

And the rain songs of all the flowering ones who have called for
the rain

can be found there, flourishing beneath the currents of singing.

Rain opens us, like flowers, or earth that has been thirsty for
more than a season.

We stop all of our talking, quit thinking, to drink the mystery.

We listen to the breathing beneath our breathing.

We hear how the rain became rain, how we became human.

The wetness saturates and cleans everything, including the
perpetrators of the second overthrow.

We will plant songs where there were curses.

We had been watching since the eve of the missionaries in their
long and solemn clothes, to see what would happen.

We saw it
from the kitchen window over the sink
as we made coffee, cooked rice and
potatoes, enough for an army.

We saw it all, as we changed diapers and fed
the babies. We saw it,
through the branches
of the knowledgeable tree
through the snags of stars, through
the sun and storms from our knees
as we bathed and washed
the floors.

The conference of the birds warned us, as they flew over
destroyers in the harbor, parked there since the first takeover.
It was by their song and talk we knew when to rise
when to look out the window
to the commotion going on—
the magnetic field thrown off by grief.

We heard it.
The racket in every corner of the world. As
the hunger for war rose up in those who would steal to be
    president
to be king or emperor, to own the trees, stones, and everything

else that moved about the earth, inside the earth
and above it.

We knew it was coming, tasted the winds who gathered
    intelligence
from each leaf and flower, from every mountain, sea
and desert, from every prayer and song all over this tiny
    universe
floating in the skies of infinite
being.

And then it was over, this world we had grown to love
for its sweet grasses, for the many-colored horses
and fishes, for the shimmering possibilities
while dreaming.

But then there were the seeds to plant and the babies
who needed milk and comforting, and someone
picked up a guitar or ukulele from the rubble
and began to sing about the light flutter
the kick beneath the skin of the earth
we felt there, beneath us

a warm animal
a song being born between the legs of her,
a poem.

FOR CALLING THE SPIRIT BACK FROM WANDERING THE EARTH IN ITS HUMAN FEET

Put down that bag of potato chips, that white bread, that bottle of pop.

Turn off that cellphone, computer, and remote control.

Open the door, then close it behind you.

Take a breath offered by friendly winds. They travel the earth gathering essences of plants to clean.

Give back with gratitude.

If you sing it will give your spirit lift to fly to the stars' ears and back.

Acknowledge this earth who has cared for you since you were a dream planting itself precisely within your parents' desire.

Let your moccasin feet take you to the encampment of the guardians who have known you before time, who will be there after time. They sit before the fire that has been there without time.

Let the earth stabilize your postcolonial insecure jitters.

Be respectful of the small insects, birds and animal people who accompany you. Ask their forgiveness for the harm we humans have brought down upon them.

Don't worry.
The heart knows the way though there may be high-rises,
interstates, checkpoints, armed soldiers, massacres, wars, and those
who will despise you because they despise themselves.

The journey might take you a few hours, a day, a year, a few years, a
hundred, a thousand or even more.

Watch your mind. Without training it might run away and leave
your heart for the immense human feast set by the thieves of time.

Do not hold regrets.

When you find your way to the circle, to the fire kept burning by the
keepers of your soul, you will be welcomed.

You must clean yourself with cedar, sage, or other healing plant.

Cut the ties you have to failure and shame.

Let go the pain you are holding in your mind, your shoulders, your
heart, all the way to your feet. Let go the pain of your ancestors to
make way for those who are heading in our direction.

Ask for forgiveness.

Call upon the help of those who love you.

Call your spirit back. It may be caught in corners and creases of
shame, judgment, and human abuse.

You must call in a way that your spirit will want to return. Speak to it as you would to a beloved child.

Welcome your spirit back from its wandering. It may return in pieces, in tatters. Gather them together. They will be happy to be found after being lost for so long.

Your spirit will need to sleep awhile after it is bathed and given clean clothes.

Now you can have a party. Invite everyone you know who loves and supports you. Keep room for those who have no place else to go.

Make a giveaway, and remember, keep the speeches short.

Then, you must do this: help the next person find their way through the dark.

In a world long before this one, there was enough for everyone,
Until somebody got out of line.
We heard it was Rabbit, fooling around with clay and wind.
Everybody was tired of his tricks and no one would play with him;
He was lonely in this world.
So Rabbit thought to make a person.
And when he blew into the mouth of the crude figure to see
What would happen,
The clay man stood up.
Rabbit showed the clay man how to steal a chicken.
The clay man obeyed.
Rabbit showed him how to steal corn.
The clay man obeyed.
Then he showed him how to steal someone else's wife.
The clay man obeyed.
Rabbit felt important and powerful.
Clay man felt important and powerful.
And once that clay man started he could not stop.
Once he took that chicken he wanted all the chickens.
And once he took that corn he wanted all the corn.
And once he took that wife, he wanted all the wives.
He was insatiable.
Then he had a taste of gold and he wanted all the gold.
Then it was land and anything else he saw.
His wanting only made him want more.
Soon it was countries, then it was trade.
The wanting infected the earth.
We lost track of the purpose and reason for life.
We began to forget our songs. We forgot our stories.

We could no longer see or hear our ancestors,
Or talk with each other across the kitchen table.
Forests were being mowed down all over the world.
And Rabbit had no place to play.
Rabbit's trick had backfired.
Rabbit tried to call the clay man back,
But when the clay man wouldn't listen
Rabbit realized he'd made a clay man with no ears.

NO

Yes, that was me you saw shaking with bravery, with a government-issued rifle on my back. I'm sorry I could not greet you, as you deserved, my relative.

They were not my tears. I have a reservoir inside. They will be cried by my sons, my daughters if I can't learn how to turn tears to stone.

Yes, that was me, standing in the back door of the house in the alley, with fresh corn and bread for the neighbors.

I did not foresee the flood of blood. How they would forget our friendship, would return to kill the babies and me.

Yes, that was me whirling on the dance floor. We made such a racket with all that joy. I loved the whole world in that silly music.

I did not realize the terrible dance in the staccato of bullets.

Yes. I smelled the burning grease of corpses. And like a fool I expected our words might rise up and jam the artillery in the hands of dictators.

We had to keep going. We sang our grief to clean the air of turbulent spirits.

Yes, I did see the terrible black clouds as I cooked dinner. And the messages of the dying spelled there in the ashy sunset. Every one addressed: "mother."

There was nothing about it in the news. Everything was the same. Unemployment was up. Another queen crowned with flowers. Then there were the sports scores.

Yes, the distance was great between your country and mine. Yet our children played in the path between our houses.

No. We had no quarrel with each other.

THIS MORNING I PRAY FOR MY ENEMIES

And whom do I call my enemy?

An enemy must be worthy of engagement.

I turn in the direction of the sun and keep walking.

It's the heart that asks the question, not my furious mind.

The heart is the smaller cousin of the sun.

It sees and knows everything.

It hears the gnashing even as it hears the blessing.

The door to the mind should only open from the heart.

An enemy who gets in, risks the danger of becoming a friend.

PRAISE THE RAIN

Praise the rain, the seagull dive
The curl of plant, the raven talk—
Praise the hurt, the house slack
The stand of trees, the dignity—
Praise the dark, the moon cradle
The sky fall, the bear sleep—
Praise the mist, the warrior name
The earth eclipse, the fired leap—
Praise the backwards, upward sky
The baby cry, the spirit food—
Praise canoe, the fish rush
The hole for frog, the upside-down—
Praise the day, the cloud cup
The mind flat, forget it all—

Praise crazy. Praise sad.
Praise the path on which we're led.
Praise the roads on earth and water.
Praise the eater and the eaten.
Praise beginnings; praise the end.
Praise the song and praise the singer.

Praise the rain; it brings more rain.
Praise the rain; it brings more rain.

SPEAKING TREE

I had a beautiful dream I was dancing with a tree.
—Sandra Cisneros

Some things on this earth are unspeakable:
Genealogy of the broken—
A shy wind threading leaves after a massacre,
Or the smell of coffee and no one there—

Some humans say trees are not sentient beings,
But they do not understand poetry—

Nor can they hear the singing of trees when they are fed by
Wind, or water music—
Or hear their cries of anguish when they are broken and
     bereft—

Now I am a woman longing to be a tree, planted in a moist,
     dark earth
Between sunrise and sunset—

I cannot walk through all realms—
I carry a yearning I cannot bear alone in the dark—

What shall I do with all this heartache?

The deepest-rooted dream of a tree is to walk
Even just a little ways, from the place next to the doorway—
To the edge of the river of life, and drink—

I have heard trees talking, long after the sun has gone down:

Imagine what would it be like to dance close together
In this land of water and knowledge . . .

To drink deep what is undrinkable.

FALL SONG

It is a dark fall day.
The earth is slightly damp with rain.
I hear a jay.
The cry is blue.
I have found you in the story again.
Is there another word for "divine"?
I need a song that will keep sky open in my mind.
If I think behind me, I might break.
If I think forward, I lose now.
Forever will be a day like this
Strung perfectly on the necklace of days.
Slightly overcast
Yellow leaves
Your jacket hanging in the hallway
Next to mine.

SUNRISE

Sunrise, as you enter the houses of everyone here, find us.
We've been crashing for days, or has it been years.
Find us, beneath the shadow of this yearning mountain, crying
    here.
We have been sick with sour longing, and the jangling of fears.
Our spirits rise up in the dark, because they hear,
Doves in cottonwoods calling forth the sun.
We struggled with a monster and lost.
Our bodies were tossed in the pile of kill.
We were ashamed and we told ourselves for a thousand years,
We didn't deserve anything but this—
And one day, in relentless eternity, our spirits discerned
    movement of prayers
Carried toward the sun.
And this morning we are able to stand with all the rest
And welcome you here.
We move with the lightness of being, and we will go
Where there's a place for us.

BREAK MY HEART

There are always flowers,
Love cries, or blood.

Someone is always leaving
By exile, death, or heartbreak.

The heart is a fist.
It pockets prayer or holds rage.

It's a timekeeper.
Music maker, or backstreet truth teller.

Baby, baby, baby
You can't say what's been said

Before, though even words
Are creatures of habit.

You cannot force poetry
With a ruler, or jail it at a desk.

Mystery is blind, but wills you
To untie the cloth, in eternity.

Police with their guns
Cannot enter here to move us off our lands.

History will always find you, and wrap you
In its thousand arms.

Someone will lift from the earth
Without wings.

Another will fall from the sky
Through the knots of a tree.

Chaos is primordial.
All words have roots here.

You will never sleep again
Though you will never stop dreaming.

The end can only follow the beginning.
And it will zigzag through time, governments, and lovers.

Be who you are, even if it kills you.

It will. Over and over again,
Even as you live.

Break my heart, why don't you?

WASHING MY MOTHER'S BODY

I never got to wash my mother's body when she died.
I return to take care of her in memory.
That's how I make peace when things are left undone.
I go back and open the door.
I step in to make my ritual. To do what should have been done,
what needs to be fixed so that my spirit can move on,
So that the children and grandchildren are not caught in a
    knot
Of regret they do not understand.

I find the white enamel pan she used to bathe us when we were
    babies.
I turn the faucet on and hold my hand under the water
until it is warm, the temperature one uses to wash an infant.
I find a clean washcloth in a stack of washcloths.
She had nothing in her childhood.
She made sure she had plenty of everything
when she grew up and made her own life.
Her closets were full of pretty dresses,
so many she had not time to wear them all.
They were bought by the young girl who wore the same flour
    sack dress
to school every day, the one she had to wash out every night,
and hang up to dry near the wood stove.

I pick up the bar of soap from her sink,
the same soap she used yesterday morning to wash her face.
When she looked in the mirror, did she know it would be her
    last sunrise?

I move over pill bottles, a clock radio on the table by the bed,
a pen, and set down the pan. I straighten the blankets over
      her,
to keep her warm, for dignity.
I start with her face. Her face is unlined even two months
      before
her eightieth birthday. She was known for her beauty,
and when younger passed for Cherokee.
My mother kept the iron pot given to her by her mother,
whose mother said it was given to her by the U.S. government
      on the Trail of Tears.
She grew flowers in it.

As I wash my mother's face, I tell her
how beautiful she is, how brave, how her beauty and bravery
live on in her grandchildren. Her face is relaxed, peaceful.
Her earth memory body has not left yet,
but when I see her the next day, embalmed and in the casket
in the funeral home, it will be gone.
Where does it go?
It is heavier than the spirit who lifted up and flew.
I think of it making the rounds to every place it has loved to say
      goodbye.
Goodbye to the house where I brought my babies home, she
      sings.
Goodbye to June's Bar where I was the shuffleboard queen.

I cannot say goodbye yet.
I will never say goodbye.

I lift up each arm to wash. Her hands still wear her favorite
    rings.
She loved her body and decorated it with shiny jewelry,
with creams and makeup.
I am tender over that burn scar on her arm,
From when she cooked at the place with the cruel boss
who insisted she reach her hand into the Fryolator to clean it.
She had protested it was still hot, and suffered a deep burn.
That scar always reminded me of her coming in
from working long hours in restaurants,
her uniform drenched with sweat, determination and
    exhaustion.
Once she came home and I was burning up with a fever.
She pulled out the same pan I am dipping the washcloth in now,
only she's added rubbing alcohol, to bring the fever down.
She washes tenderly, tells me about how her friend Chunkie
left her husband again, how she knows her old boss,
a Jewish woman who treated her kindly,
has cancer. She doesn't know how she knows;
she just knows.
She doesn't tell me that—
I find it in a journal she has left me,
a day book in which she has written notes
for me to find when she is gone.

I wash her neck, lift the blankets to move down to her heart.
I thank her body for carrying us through the tough story,
through the violence of my father, and her second husband.

The story is all there, in her body, as I wash her to prepare her
to be let down into earth, and return all stories to the earth.

My body memories rise up as I wash.
I recall carrying my two children, rocking them,
and feeding them from my body.
How I knew myself as beloved Earth, in that body.

I uncover my mother's legs.
I remember the varicose veins that swelled like rivers
when my mother would get off a long shift of standing and
    cooking.
They carried more than a woman should carry.
A woman should be honored like a queen,
traditionally we treated our women with that kind of respect,
my Creek husband tells me.
Ha, I laugh and ask him, "then why aren't you cooking my
    dinner?"
I wash her feet, caress them.
You will have some rest now, I tell my mother,
even as I know my mother was never one for resting.
I cover her.

I make the final wring of the washcloth and drape it over the
    pan.
I brush my mother's hair and kiss her forehead.
I ask the keepers of the journey to make sure her travel is safe
    and sure.
I ask the angels, whom she loved and with whom she spoke
    frequently,
to take her home, but wait, not before I find her favorite
    perfume.
Then I sing her favorite song, softly.
I don't know the name of the song, just a few phrases,

one of those old homemade heartbreak songs
where there's a moment of happiness
wound through—

and then I let her go.

HOW TO WRITE A POEM IN A TIME OF WAR

You can't begin just anywhere. It's a wreck.

Shrapnel and the eye

of a house, a row of houses. There's a rat scrambling

from light with fleshy trash in its mouth. A baby strapped

to its mother's back, cut loose.

Soldiers crawl the city,

the river, the town, the village,

the bedroom, our kitchen. They eat everything.

Or burn it.

They kill what they cannot take. They rape. What they cannot
kill they take.

Rumors fall like rain.

Like bombs.

Like mother and father tears

swallowed for restless peace.

Like sunset slanting toward a moonless midnight.

Like a train blown free of its destination.   Like a seed

fallen where

there is no chance of trees   or anyplace   for birds to live.

No, start here.   Deer peer from the edge of the woods.

                                                We used to see woodpeckers

the size of the sun, and were greeted

                        by chickadees with their good morning songs.

We'd started to cook outside, slippery with dew and laughter,

                                ah these smoky sweet sunrises.

We tried to pretend war wasn't going to happen.

Though they began building their houses all around us

                                        and demanding more.

They started teaching our children their god's story,

                        a story in which we'd always be slaves.

No. Not here.

You can't begin here.

This is memory shredded because it is impossible to hold with words,

        even poetry.

These memories were left here with the trees.

The torn pocket of your daughter's hand-sewn dress,

    the sash, the lace.

The baby's delicately beaded moccasin still connected to her
    foot,

a young man's note of promise to his beloved—

            No! This is not the best place to begin.

Everyone was asleep, despite the distant bombs.

         Terror had become the familiar stranger.

Our beloved twin girls curled up in their nightgowns,

            next to their father and me.

If we begin here, none of us will make it to the end

of the poem.

Someone has to make it out alive, sang a grandfather

to his grandson, his granddaughter,

as he blew his most powerful song into the hearts of the
      children.

There it would be hidden from the soldiers,

who would take them miles, rivers, mountains

                        from the navel cord place of the origin story.

He knew one day, far day, the grandchildren would return,

generations later over slick highways constructed over old trails

through walls of laws meant to hamper or destroy, over stones

bearing libraries of the winds.

He sang us back

            to our home place from which we were stolen

                        in these smoky green hills.

Yes, begin here.

RUNNING

It's closing time. Violence is my boyfriend
With a cross to bear
                Hoisted on by the church.
He wears it everywhere.
There are no female deities in the Trinity.
       I don't know how I'm going to get out of here,
Said the flying fish to the tree.
                     Last call.
We've had it with history, we who look for vision here
In the Indian and poetry bar, somewhere
To the left of Hell.
Now I have to find my way, when there's a river to cross and no
Boat to get me there, when there appears to be no home at all.
                         My father gone, chased
By the stepfather's gun. *Get out of here.*
I've found my father at the bar, his ghost at least, some piece
Of him in this sorry place. The boyfriend's convincing to a crowd.
Right now, he's the spell of attraction. What tales he tells.
In the fog of thin hope, I wander this sad world
We've made with the enemy's words.
The lights quiver,
       Like they do when the power's dwindling to a dangling
          string.
It is time to go home. We are herded like stoned cattle, like
      children for the bombing drill—
                  Out the door, into the dark street of this old
                  Indian town
Where there are no Indians anymore.
I was afraid of the dark, because then I could see

Everything. The truth with its eyes staring
Back at me. The mouth of the dark with its shiny moon teeth,
No words, just a hiss and a snap.

I could hear my heart hurting
With my *in-the-dark ears*.

I thought I could take it. Where was the party?
It's been a century since we left home with the American
    soldiers at our backs.
The party had long started up in the parking lot.
He flew through the dark, broke my stride with a
        punch.
I went down then came up.

I thought I could take being a girl with her heart in her
Arms. I carried it for justice. For the rights of all Indians.
We all had that cross to bear.
Those Old Ones followed me, the quiet girl with the long dark
    hair,
The daughter of a warrior who wouldn't give up.
I wasn't ready yet, to fling free the cross

I ran and I ran through the 2 a.m. streets.

It was my way of breaking free. I was anything but history.
I was the wind.

MY MAN'S FEET

They are heroic roots
You cannot mistake them
For any other six-foot walker
I could find them in a sea of feet
A planet or universe of feet

They kicked the sky at birth
In that town his great-grandfather found
My man's feet left childhood
Past the mineral grit of an oil flush bust
To these atomic eastbound lands

His feet are made of his mother's spiritual concern
And of his father: historic, and mindfully upright
What walkers—
From mound builder steps that led to the sky maker
Past Spanish galleons, stage coach, and railroad snaker

One generation following another
No other feet but these could bare
The rock stubborn loyal bear
Towering intelligence and children picker upper
That is the one who owns these feet

What an anchor his feet provide
For his unmatched
Immensability and get up againality

I've danced behind this man in the stomp dance circle
Our feet beating rhythm together
Man, woman, boy, girl, sun and moon jumper

My man's feet are the sure steps of a father
Looking after his sons, his daughters
For when he laughs he opens all the doors of our hearts
Even as he forgets to shut them when he leaves

And when he grieves for those he loves
He carves out valleys enough to hold everyone's tears
With his feet, these feet
My man's widely humble, ever steady, beautiful brown feet.

TOBACCO ORIGIN STORY

It was way back, before there was a way back
When time threaded earth and sky
Children were conceived, were born, grew, and walked tall
In what we now call a day.
Every planted thought grew plant
Ladders to the stars, way back, before there was
No way back, *Miss Mary Mack*
We used to sing along the buttons of her
Dress. Our babies are always
Our babies. Even back then when time waved through
The corn. We knew our plants like
Relatives. Their stories were our stories, there
Were songs for everything then,
For every transformation
For that first couple, a young Mvskoke man
And woman, who walked through the
Shimmer of the early evening.
They had become as one song.
They lay down when it was dark. I can hear their
Intimate low-voice talking
How they tease one another with such gut love.
Earth makes a bed, with pillow
Mounds. And it is there as the night insects sing
They conceived their first child. They
Will look back as they walk East toward the sunrise
The raw stalks of beginning
Will drink the light, root deeply dark into earth.
In the tracks of their loving
The plant child emerges, first the seed head, then

Leafy, long male body and the white female
Flowers of tobacco, or
Hece, as the people called it when it called
To them. *Come here. We were brought*
To you from those who love you. We will help you.
And that's how it began, way
Back, when we knew how to hear the songs of plants
And could sing back, like now
On paper, with marks like bird feet, but where are
Our ears? They have grown to fit
Around earbuds, to hear music made for cold
Cash, like our beloved smoke—
Making threaded with addiction and dead words.
Sing this song back to me girl.
In the moonlight tobacco plant had silver
Moon buttons all up her back.
We're getting dressed to go plant new songs with words.
Our sun is dimming faster.
Mvto hece, mvto hvse, mvto—
Ekvnvcakv, mvto ah

REDBIRD LOVE

We watched her grow up.
She was the urgent chirper,
Fledgling flier.
And when spring rolled
Out its green
She'd grown
Into the most noticeable
Bird-girl.
Long-legged and just
The right amount of blush
Tipping her wings, crest
And tail, and
She knew it
In the bird parade.
We watched her strut.
She owned her stuff.
The males perked their armor, greased their wings,
And flew sky-loop missions
To show off
For her.
In the end
There was only one.
There's that one you circle back to—for home.
This morning
The young couple scavenge seeds
On the patio.
She is thickening with eggs.
Their minds are busy with sticks the perfect size, tufts of fluff
Like dandelion, and other pieces of soft.

He steps aside for her, so she can eat.
Then we watch him fill his beak
Walk tenderly to her and kiss her with seed.
The sacred world lifts up its head
To notice—
We are double, triple blessed.

AN AMERICAN SUNRISE

We were running out of breath, as we ran out to meet ourselves. We
Were surfacing the edge of our ancestors' fights, and ready to Strike
It was difficult to lose days in the Indian bar if you were Straight.
Easy if you played pool and drank to remember to forget. We
Made plans to be professional—and did. And some of us could Sing
When we drove to the edge of the mountains, with a drum. We
Made sense of our beautiful crazed lives under the starry stars. Sin
Was invented by the Christians, as was the Devil, we sang. We
Were the heathens, but needed to be saved from them: Thin
Chance. We knew we were all related in this story, a little Gin
Will clarify the dark, and make us all feel like dancing. We
Had something to do with the origins of blues and Jazz
I argued with the music as I filled the jukebox with dimes in June,

Forty years later and we still want justice. We are still America. We.

FROG IN A DRY RIVER

When you talk with the dead
You can only go as far as the edge of the bank.

I heard more than one frog singing.

She came to me more than once in dead
Sleep. We used to drink, and she doesn't want anyone to tell.

I met the king of the frogs once perched on the lip of the ditch.

The water had been let down for the summer for the crops
And we camped out nearby, with singers, the ones who knew
The oldest songs.

Said the frog as he pitched his favorite pillow behind his
Aching back

It's hard getting old, and soon we will all be dead.
He sang as we sat together and watched
The human traffic hiking by.

The jealousy beast lives too among us frogs, he mused.

I watched it going across in a yellow boat, toward the
Land of the dead. It had six rowers to haul the sharp-tongued.

We are never free of ourselves, not here or in froggy heaven.

Then the river spoke up. She'd had enough of the disregard,

The theft. *I'm not dead*, she said.

I wanted to learn a song from the frog. The frog leaped in, and
My mind followed. I started this poem.

To argue with the living is hard enough, forget the dead.
I will end here, instead.

PREPARE

You are a story fed by generations
You carry songs of grief, triumph
Loss and joy
Feel their power as they ascend
Within you
As you walk, run swiftly, even fly
Into infinite possibilities

Let go that which burdens you
Let go any acts of unkindness or brutality
From or against you
Let go that which has burdened your family
Your community, your nation
Or disturbed your soul
Let go one breath into another

Pray thankfulness for this Earth we are
For this becoming we are
For this sunlight touching skin we are
For the cooling of the dark we are

Listen now as Earth sheds her skin
Listen as generations move
One against the other to make power
We are bringing in a new story

We will be accompanied by ancient songs
And will celebrate together

Breathe this new dawn
Assist it as it opens its mouth
To sing.

THE LIFE OF BEAUTY

The sung blessing of creation
Led her into the human story.
That was the first beauty.

Next beauty was the sound of her mother's voice
Rippling the waters beneath the drumming skin
Of her birthing cocoon.

Next beauty the father with kindness in his hands
As he held the newborn against his breathing.

Next beauty the moon through the dark window,
It was a rocking horse, a wish.

There were many beauties in this age
For everything was immensely itself:
Green greener than the impossibility of green,
The taste of wind after its slide through dew grass at dawn,
Or language running through a tangle of wordlessness in her
Mouth.

She ate well of the next beauty.

Next beauty planted itself urgently beneath the warrior shrines.

Next was beauty beaded by her mother and pinned neatly
To hold back her hair.

Then tendrils of her fire longing grew into her, beautiful
The flower between her legs as she became herself.

Do not forget this beauty she was told.

The story took her far away from beauty. In the tests of her
    living,
Beauty was often long from the reach of her mind and spirit.
When she forgot beauty, all was brutal.
But beauty always came to lift her up to stand again.

When it was beautiful all around and within,
She knew herself to be corn plant, moon, and sunrise.

Death is beautiful, she sang, as she left this story behind her.

Even her bones, said time,
Were tuned to beauty.

HOW LOVE BLOWS THROUGH THE TREES

This old Creek town appears empty except for the trees
And the story of how wind will come to clean
The earth, of the takers who took
And never give back.
One day, my grandfather used to sing
A fresh world will rise up
To take the place of a society
That didn't love the earth.

We lost ourselves when we crossed the river
My grandfather used to say.
He would smoke to the east, north, west, and south
And touch the earth and the sky.
He'd be standing in the kitchen
And there'd be no one listening.

Pass this love on, he'd say.
It knows how to bend and will never break.
It's the only thing with a give and take,
The more it's used the more it makes.

My grandfather flew like smoke to the sky side of earth.
He left us here in this place he blessed.
What stories he carried, what laughter-wrapped memory.
Now I'm standing in the kitchen
And I can hear him singing,
Sometimes it takes a while for us to hear.

Pass this love on, he'd say.
It knows how to bend and will never break.
It's the only thing with a give and take,
The more it's used the more it makes.

That love is the bridge that will cross the river home.
He'd be standing in the dark with no one listening.
How time blows steadily through the city, the trees.
Sing to this earth, sing, he sang.

SUNDOWN WALKS TO THE EDGE OF THE STORY

In the lands of forgotten memories,
I hear a woman singing.
A dog runs in circles, barking.
Then children laugh as they run through,
The sashes of one girl's dress are dragging
On the ground from playing horse.

In this story is a woman with a husband she adores.
He is the color of warm brown earth, tall,
With kind eyes that shine with love for her.
When he loves it is with every part of his body
From his planted feet to his head good with numbers.

When she first lay down with him, their love made roots
That dove into the ground, caressed the stones.
These roots find water where water is needed.

Those nights of early love, he spoke to her when she was
    sleeping.
His words were the vision of an architect of good dreams.
He told her how he would treasure her, how they would walk
Through this life to the next with each other, no matter
The tests and disappointments that befall a human
On this earthly road.

Those words blossomed into flowers, waters, and sunrises.
She wears each day as a river pearl in a necklace, though the
    pearls
Darken with age, they never let up their glow.

Time is nothing in those lands.
It has been years.
They lay down together to sleep, in their grown old bones,
Their weathered skins.
She is a woman made of words.
He is a man now impatient with words.
They hold hands in the dark and fall asleep together.

I find them, as sundown walks to the edge of the story
To wait for sunrise. I find them in a song sung about a woman
Weeping with joy, about a man whose love for her
Does not need words but contains every color
That love has ever worn.

SOMEWHERE

It was the day of brutal winds, all of them ganging up to blow injustice down. They sang the changing weather. I was going nowhere.

Anything on the ground not burdened by gravity was twisted and lifted up to drop. There were dreams, cities, and plastic bags. I was going nowhere.

I tightened my coat to the approaching winter, but you cannot duel and win against a season, history, or a murder of winds.

Shooting down MLK Boulevard, I was approaching Archer, the juncture of several histories. A burned street of wishes was smoking there. I was going nowhere.

I just wanted to get home, but where is home I always ask the sky, no matter where I roam. An old Mvskoke map is different. We know by trees, rocks, and the obligations of relatives. We might be going nowhere.

Our roads aren't nice lines with numbers; they wind like bloodlines through gossip and stories of the holy in the winds. History is everywhere. Three tribal nations met here. We weren't going to go anywhere.

At the corner of justice and fight, the thought of the miraculous was miles from my mind. It was nowhere in my mind. It was curled up in a distant field in the heart of a once-loved country.

Then I saw books flying from an unseen woman's hands, shoes that never fit her or anyone, and poetry everywhere. She was going nowhere.

I had been thinking of the massacre down the street from here, and how ghosts keep their place among us. How I might be a ghost set loose here in the wind, walking with a ghost of fire.

And then there she stood, a ruined goddess, half-naked on the sidewalk, classic Africa in her stance of beauty. We are going nowhere.

"Excuse me, excuse me," she called out to me. There is no excuse for this raw story of abuse. And no clothes will fit this moment of the tale. Nothing good enough for her beauty.

She was a child when she was first taken. Her home is her pain naked without clothes. Where was her father, her mother? Burning. There is nowhere nowhere.

Time is always moving. It is we blood carriers who stay rooted to the gravity of hurt. The story has to be told to be free like a tree lifted in a breeze. If we don't tell it, the stillness will.

I could give her my jeans, my jacket, my shoes. I searched her mind as it flew in the wind. My mind chased her mind through tunnels of time. It was going nowhere.

There is no excuse, sang the winds of forgotten history as they covered her up with a ragged blanket stitched with loneliness to take her with them.

I was feeling my pockets for change, for guns to protect her, nails and lumber to rebuild all the houses burned by hatred. I only found a pen without paper. History goes nowhere.

It is always female power that bears truth to righteousness of any new nation. Liberty guards the harbor. Sacagawea the river of discovery. The Virgen de Guadalupe, the earth.

And here, the one for whom I have no name, is not nameless. The mass grave is a grave of names. Without knowing them, we are going nowhere.

I see her now on every corner, the miracle the winds brought, a song made by the rejects of history, wearing clothes that cover nothing. She is everywhere.

I turn up the music. It's from my girlhood just miles up the road. Blood tales run through our bones, like these streets made of the unspeakable. These winds will never stop telling the truth. I thought I was going nowhere.

WITHOUT

The world will keep trudging through time without us

When we lift from the story contest to fly home

We will be as falling stars to those watching from the edge

Of grief and heartbreak

Maybe then we will see the design of the two-minded creature

And know why half the world fights righteously for greedy
    masters

And the other half is nailing it all back together

Through the smoke of cooking fires, lovers' trysts, and endless

Human industry—

Maybe then, beloved rascal

We will find each other again in the timeless weave of breathing

We will sit under the trees in the shadow of earth sorrows

Watch hyenas drink rain, and laugh.

NOTES

The Last Song (page 1)

This was one of the earliest poems, the lead poem of my first book, a chapbook of poems and original drawings. I was a student at the University of New Mexico, just discovering poetry. I was surprised at how poetry began to displace making art as my primary means of expression. Every poem became a kind of doorway to questioning, even as many of the poems were written with words as tools to express awe. My generation of Native students was motivated by social justice, yet, if I consider it, every generation of Native students since the arrival of the settlers must have been asking the same questions, having witnessed acts of injustice. Simply being indigenous in cultural institutions that were centered in ideas, forms, and structures brought to supplant their peoples meant being witness to injustice, as education was and often remains a colonizing tool to destroy peoples and cultures.

The question every Native student in my generation asked of newcomers and visitors was "Where you from?" Because the university was in Albuquerque, most students were Navajo, Pueblo, or Apache. There were a few of us from Oklahoma or other faraway places, from Native Nations with different histories and cultures. In our work for justice, we traveled together all over the southwestern reservations and sometimes into other states. This poem was from a conversation with a Navajo, or Diné, student. Many of my earliest poems originated from overheard conversations. We were being urged in our writing workshops to speak naturally.

My favorite summer music is from insect orchestras. The small stones in our shells and/or cans when we dance resonate with those insect songs. We feel ourselves part of the larger earth song.

The Chilean poet Pablo Neruda was an influence, or poetry ancestor, of this poem.

Are You Still There? (page 2)

In those earliest times of my poetry writing, in the early 1970s, the women's movement had emerged as a national political force, even as far away as Albuquerque, on the University of New Mexico campus. We needed massive changes in thought and practice about women and female power. We fought for changes in the overculture (the American consumer society) regarding women's respective and crucial place in our societies, though the way Native women approached this was in many ways different from the European American women who led the challenge. In our original teachings women are seen as integral to life.

In our Mvskoke culture, women are meant to be side by side with men, each, at their best, made for balance in the world. But that natural law was perverted by those in places of power who strove to keep women kneeling at the bottom of a hierarchy in subservience and shame. As our Native peoples came up in religious and governmental institutions, they were educated by that hierarchical measure, a measure in which women and Native peoples would always be at the bottom. Our female deities were cast aside.

Though my mother was one of the strongest human beings I knew, I saw her threatened and give in to the power structure and to those upholding the repressive architecture, to survive. I discovered that the act of writing and creating is a dual power. It opens a pathway outward and at the same time inward. In that conversation of the poem, that relationship, I gave away my power, even as the poem enabled me to hold it up to the light to clearly see the heartbreak.

I often felt voiceless because I didn't feel like I fit anywhere precisely. I was coming to poetry in a community in which I was more on the outside than the inside because of my tribal affiliation and my mixed-cultural heritage. I allowed the anxiety to silence me.

When I took back my power, it disrupted a family system. I learned how to give voice to that within myself, and by doing so helped make a path for others to lift up their voices.

Anchorage (page 3)

To make a living as a poet with a family to raise, I was open to economic opportunity. The Laguna Pueblo novelist and poet Leslie Marmon Silko often sent work my way. Once she was asked to write a screenplay for a project with the White River Apache Tribe. She couldn't do it, but maybe I could. Of course, I said yes. My response wasn't only economic, I was excited about writing the story, and did, with assistance from books on how to write a screenplay and advice from a known and respected screenwriter. This was before YouTube and the Internet made access to learning easier.

I also participated as poet-in-residence in many poetry-in-the-schools programs in Oklahoma, New Mexico, and Arizona. When I was approached and asked to participate in a similar program in Alaska for those in prisons and jails, I agreed. I had never been as far away as Anchorage, Alaska. I had gone to Indian school with several Alaskan Natives. I knew that nationally a very high percentage of the populations of prisons and jails were of Native people.

Because I had no credit cards I could only rent from Rent-A-Wreck. They took cash deposits. They gave me a refurbished police car. With poetry under my arm, I visited four penal institutions for men in and around Anchorage, and one for women.

This poem came from my first visit, which was the Fourth Avenue jail. I didn't know what to expect. I was led in by the jailer to a room with a seminar table. Inmates sat around it. The jailer said, "I'll be back in two hours," then he shut and locked the door from the outside. My curiosity for this new situation and interest in these men and their lives and love for poetry kept my mind away from any fear about being locked in a room as a young woman with several incarcerated inmates. Reading and speaking poetry made for an intimate circle. We told stories. Many of the inmates knew poetry by heart. We read and wrote poetry. There were many tears, and even laughter. All of us were just trying to find our way through a system that did not support our cultures, our humanity.

Every poem has ancestors. Audre Lorde's poem "A Litany for Survival" is echoed in the last lines, following Henry's story that burned impossible but true.

For Alva Benson, and for Those Who Have Learned to Speak (page 5)
I think of this poem as an honoring song. My urge to write poetry began as I searched for words to find a healing path, as our University of New Mexico Native student organization, the Kiva Club, worked for justice in our tribal communities. We battled city, state, and national inequities, even as we called out corporations for theft of coal, oil, and uranium from our lands. As we

united for these battles, battles that took place in meetings, on paper, and in marches to show solidarity and make change, we were tested personally and collectively.

One young woman stood out to me. In those years, not so many women with children attended the university as they do now. I remember one Navajo woman showing up at our meetings with her five well-behaved children in tow. They were always neatly dressed, the boys' hair slicked down, the girls wearing their hair in the traditional tsiiyééł style, bound up with colored yarn. I knew how stressed I was with raising two children with little to no help. Back then, you were not given extra loans or scholarship funds for children. Another woman, also Navajo, Alva Benson, was part of the backbone of our organization. She was always helping with whatever tasks were needed, like copying and leafleting, and was a crucial presence at our events. I don't remember her speaking much. Her actions and manner of actions spoke of a deeply embedded sense of grace and purpose. She had a daughter whom she cared for diligently. I can remember her laugh, as the women would stand together joking after our meetings.

This poem was my way of remembering her. I did not want to forget her, her part in our efforts and those times, which, while faded, are still crucial to where we stand now as Native Nations in this country.

She passed from this life before graduation from an accident. I don't remember what it was exactly. We mourned her and missed her quiet, steady presence.

Women, like the earth, are the carriers of nourishment and beauty. She will always exemplify this for me.

The Woman Hanging from the Thirteenth-Floor Window (page 7)
I remember how this poem started. I was in my office at the Institute of American Indian Arts when I first taught there in 1978–1979. I was at my desk, writing on my typewriter. When I write I follow dreams and thoughts. I investigate memories, some of them not mine. I use words, sound, and rhythm to find my way. I do not know where the journey will take me, or exactly how I will get there. I enjoy the winds, the plants, the kinds of animals that might appear along the way. I like the ability to weave with time, to play with time.

I kept returning in my memory to the trip to Chicago I took with my children when I was a student at the University of Iowa. We went to visit my friend Sandra Cisneros. We had never been to a city of that size. We took in the sights, like the Sears Tower, the lakefront, and the Field Museum of Natural History's King Tut exhibit. We also visited the American Indian Center of Chicago. Wherever it was we traveled, we always checked out where Natives lived and congregated.

It was a rocking chair in the American Indian Center that kept pulling me back in memory. Once I imagined two little girls who rocked and turned the chair as they waited for their mother who was speaking to the social worker. Another time, an older man from one of those Wisconsin tribes sat in the chair, singing songs that were to be passed to his grandchildren who were not there. Finally, as I sat in my office, looking out the window at the tall cottonwoods, there was a woman about my age or a little older who sat in the rocking chair. She would not leave. She told me, "I am not leaving until you tell my story." That's when the poem began to find its way.

There is no east Chicago.

There is usually no thirteenth floor in tall buildings.

Remember (page 10)

I hadn't been writing long when I wrote this poem. I believe I was still a student at the University of New Mexico. My first few poems were published in the *Thunderbird*, the student literary magazine. My voice found itself, then rooted itself in the Sandia Mountains, the Rio Grande River, in the sunrises and sunsets of the Southwest. My voice found a place to eat and drink after traveling through worlds and walking through time, a place to replicate the sense of those worlds in words. That's when I began writing poetry, real poetry, after those first few published poems. Those first attempts were my calling out for poetry to find me.

My first poems were often shorter and image driven. I wrote as a single young mother who worked, went to school, and attempted to raise children far from any family help. I most often wrote at night, after cooking, washing dishes, tending to the children. Soon it was my occupation. I immersed myself in the world of poetry. I attended poetry readings; I read, studied, and listened to poetry. I began building a reputation as a poet as an undergraduate student.

Someone requested that I write a poem for younger Native poets coming up. That is the poem, "Remember." It has traveled farther than any other poem I have written. It is now on its way to Jupiter's asteroid field, via NASA's *Lucy* space probe, which was launched in October 2021.

New Orleans (page 11)

My first trip to the South, in the direction of our Mvskoke homelands, was in the late seventies or early eighties, when I traveled to New Orleans to be a panelist for a meeting of the Coordinating Council of Literary Magazines (or CCLM). I appreciated the opportunity to read and see what was being published in the larger literary world and to meet and discuss with the other panelists, all people I respected. What also excited me was that I was on the other side of the Mississippi River, the river my people crossed on our forced march from our homelands. This was the closest I'd come to our home. I took in everything in that town as we took breaks from our discussions: the French- and Spanish-influenced architecture, the dank air of river meeting sky, and the layers of history moving like winds through that city.

I imagine that most of this poem resides in the unspoken.

As I write this, I remember the scholar Kathleen Sands, who taught at Arizona State University. She was an early champion of this poem, of my poetry. She was one of the first academics to write about this poem, to take me seriously as a poet.

She Had Some Horses (page 14)

I remember that drafty house in Santa Fe, and the corner where I sat at my desk to write. Or, it was another place I lived with my children, my children who moved with me from one apartment or house to the other to accommodate my jobs, my wandering. We were near an intersection, so it was noisy. They went to school that day and I remember the slant of the sun as it moved across my hands on the typewriter. I followed that poem.

I do not know how it started, but I know the poem's roots: Navajo horse songs, my great-grandfather's horse magic, a need to speak about the contradictions within ourselves, a need of something unspeakable.

I mimicked repetition in song forms.

I let the poem take me beyond the words.

That's when it happened.

For me, it is rhythm I catch on to, whether I am writing poetry, music, or any other kind of form. Rhythm is patterning and design. It gives shape and makes a path for intention to ride, even on horseback. It is often rhythm that captures me. I am a kinetic writer who mines the senses, even as I overanalyze and often give my mind a task to do to get it out of the way. For instance, "Mind, please open the door of the imagination and keep it open for this little while." Then, when I am ready for heavy revision, I motion it over to its work.

I need to mention here that the poem didn't just happen in one draft. I understand revision as a kind of call-and-response even as it's a balancing of elements so the meaning fits and can move backward and forward.

I Give You Back (page 17)

This poem is an incantation that I needed to literally survive. The poem came to me during a terrifying period of my life. I appeared okay because I had to be. I was the only one there in the day-to-day for my children. Something broke in me. I do not know how to describe this and do not want to attempt to describe it, as I don't want the destructive force to feel it has a structure and a place to live. I endured what was essentially a breakdown, yet I got up, tended to everything quietly and steadily as I made my way through the routine of my life.

I fought daily for my life even as I fought to have enough money to feed my children. I fought off my ex, who threatened to kill me because I wouldn't stay with him, and I fought off the demons who dangled suicide as an easy way out as they wrestled me for control of my life. I did not have words to describe it, nor did I have anyone I could speak to about what was happening. I had to go on, and I did.

Poetry gave me words to speak what had no words. Poetry stood by me. I read the poetry of Okot p'Bitek. I read Audre Lorde and *The Black Poets* by Dudley Randall. I read Leslie Marmon Silko and Adrienne Rich. The singing of Theodore Roethke turned over and over in my mind.

This poem came somewhere in the fight. I wanted to live. I wanted my children to have a mother. I wanted to fulfill the promise of this gift of life. I had fought hard for my life at birth, even as I was dying, and I was fighting again. This poem gave me an anchor. It called out fear.

Eventually I was free.

My House Is the Red Earth (page 19)

This poem is constructed of a trio of poetic prose pieces that accompanied photographic images by the astronomer and photographer Stephen Strom in our collaboration, *Secrets from the Center of the World*. The pieces were written to give back the beauty and mystery in those southwestern lands that captivated both the photographer and me. I have traveled all over the Four Corners area, and the lands of the tribal nations of the Diné, or Navajo, people, the Pueblo, and Apache. I heard many of the stories that go along with these land formations. I thought of collecting those stories and writing them down, then realized I wasn't the person to do so. These poems were a giveback so they would know how much I appreciate the lands and the forms that populate them. These lands hold time in a very particular way. They make me want to sing.

Grace (page 20)

There was a moment when I understood grace. It had been one of the coldest winters on record in Iowa City, where I was attending the Iowa Writers' Workshop in the late seventies. I marked sunless days on the calendar. (I come from a sun culture.) They extended over a month. These were also days of the long nights. I felt far away from the familiar. Even my words, my use of language, felt distant from me, and I did not know who I was there in that place of flat, rolling lands of cornfields. I could not find my grounding. Then, one morning, after waiting for a table at a Perkins Cake & Steak in Coralville, light came in and slanted across the booth where I had landed with friends who were also seeking refuge in a strange land after a long night. For a moment, in that light, the journey felt perfect.

Deer Dancer (page 21)

This is a storytelling poem, told from a story told to me by someone who was in that Milwaukee Indian bar the night the young Indian woman came in, so burdened by her story that she had to lay it down in a most striking manner. We can't carry everything, though we might try because we love our family and our people, and because history is heavy in those whose roots are deepest in these lands. The contrast between the coldest night of the year and the spare body of a young woman who strips to a storytelling song on the jukebox, because she had no other way to speak, haunts me. I never know where a poem will lead me, and this one led me back through our Mvskoke stories to the Deer Woman stories. There is not an exact correlation here, rather a similar echo. It is told that Deer Woman steals men who are misbehaving in the community. She is attractive and they will dance with her then follow her into the woods.

For Anna Mae Pictou Aquash (page 24)

This is a poem of grief, for a beloved figure in the Native social justice community in the mid- to late seventies. She was a young mother with two children who sacrificed to work at the frontlines of the American Indian Movement (AIM). My version of the story, given the details I have heard from those in and around AIM who knew Anna Mae, was that she was a victim of jealousy. She was one of the few visible women. She was beautiful, personable, and a hard worker. The FBI had been coming around asking questions of her and rumors accumulated that she might be an informer. Everyone who knew Anna Mae knew there was no truth to the rumors. Someone inside AIM ordered her killed. Her body was found during the spring melt, her raped and tortured body was found tossed in a ditch by a rancher fixing his fences. The first coroner pronounced her dead of alcohol and exposure. The coroner brought in by those in the social justice community who knew Anna Mae found a small-caliber gunshot wound in her head. The truth of history will always emerge. For Anna Mae, justice will eventually find her way.

Bird (page 26)

Though the roots of jazz, just like the roots of these lands, are ancient and deep, jazz as an artform isn't that old, just as this country is a very young country. I've always admired Charlie Parker, the harbinger of bebop. In his music he was innovative, fast. His arpeggios were wily cascading notes. Yet, his personal life challenged his artistry.

Every movie adaption of a player's life is always an interpretation, a wedge made from the particular attention of the writer, director, and actors. Clint Eastwood is a jazz man, even as he has made his name as an actor and a director. His exploration of Charlie Parker's life moved through the chaos of this groundbreaking musician's becoming. Because of this theatrical storytelling we see one version of how "Bird" became Bird.

Genius is difficult to carry. No one understands and even the artist doesn't fully comprehend the gift and what it requires. It is very demanding. Add to that being a Black man in America and the road is made even more treacherous. It was the music that held tight to the center even as it explored the edge. When I walked out of the movie theater into a dry Tucson desert night after watching the film *Bird* I was filled "out to here" (then and now) with Parker's music, stunned by how his solos defied gravity. There are many failures that go into a high-wire act. His horn was how he kept going, even when it killed him.

Rainy Dawn (page 28)

When my brilliant, quiet, perceptive girl was turning thirteen I foresaw our struggles, our challenges. Becoming a woman is one of the most powerful transformative acts. It is empowering even as it is dangerous. When I studied the maternal female line of becoming, I observed the pitfalls. Our becoming was similarly marked by stubbornness, creativity, and independence. I decided to write a poem that would be an anchor in the storm.

At every birthday we recall the story of birth for the celebrant. For instance, with my daughter I was in false labor for a week or so and then early one morning the contractions appeared to take hold. Her father and I walked to the corner of Yale and Central in Albuquerque to get a bus, then caught a taxi. We had no car. When I was checked in, then wheeled to the labor room, my labor stopped. It started up again. My view was the parking lot. It was a very hot day. That afternoon it was time. She took a breath and her spirit expanded in her tiny body. One of her father's best poems is about how when she was born, her first breath was as if sunrise moved through her. He sang of how sunrise changes the colors of the land as it moves to the horizon and above it. Soon I held the gift of her in my arms.

We made it through. She was named "Rainy Dawn" because she is of the desert and rain is one of the most precious gifts to desert earth. The poem then can also be used to bring rain.

Santa Fe (page 29)

This poem marked my prose poem phase. And I was influenced by Surrealism. The Surrealists were always highlighted in my early courses in poetry at the university, especially those taught by one of my mentors, Gene Frumkin. I was especially moved by the poetry of Federico García Lorca. A poem by Lorca functions as an extended metaphor, or rather as metaphoric waves of perception. Often his poems are constructed of seemingly incongruent images that stack into staggering meaning that break your heart. Though my poem is prosaic, there is inner form, a kind of zigzag of consciousness moving through that city where my poetry was born, just as I wandered there as a young woman, collecting memories and images.

Eagle Poem (page 30)

This poem was given to me by the eagles. They circled over the sweat tent as we emerged one day, after cleaning ourselves with prayers, stories, hot stones, and plants. There were four of them. We see you, we said, and we thanked them for their message that assured us that though our challenges were many we would continue our path that would eventually return us home, the home we left when we fell from the sky and came down to earth.

I needed this poem, and I was not the only one. I came to realize that it was a prayer, given to assist with the journey. It has been used in many funerals, on birth announcements, and at marriage and other ceremonial events. It is a blessing by the eagles, passed on through words that were given to me. As the poet, I make a structure for the meaning to live. I use words, rhythm, metaphor, syntax, and music. And time. Time is a major tool to craft meaning in a poem.

That event of the circling eagles took place in the very early eighties. They are still circling, in memory, in the poem. They are still blessing us.

The Creation Story (page 31)

There are times in our lives when we are blown open by events and the door won't close, no matter how hard you push. The vulnerability is nearly unbearable. This can happen with grief, with a breakup, with the breaking of a country that you love. In these times, I go to poetry. I walk through the woods of heartache in a poem. In those woods I can cry out and not disturb anyone. I can curl up, cover myself with earth, and sleep the sleep that evades me in those times.

A Postcolonial Tale (page 33)

I revised the original version of this poem to add song elements. I recorded it with my band Joy Harjo and Poetic Justice on the album *Letter from the End of the Twentieth Century*. I often get asked about the writing of poems versus the writing of lyrics, and what of the crossover? Each poem is different, has its own coming of age story. I adapted the original version of the poem to a reggae-style song. Song forms often include a chorus. I then made a chorus that works in the poem as a repeating stanza:

When we fell, we were not aware of falling. We were driving to work, or to the mall. The children were in school learning subtraction with guns.

I admit I have a stuck point with sunrises, the East, and creation stories. I am thinking that from this shifting vantage point of fifty years of writing, it might change to sunsets, the West, and stories of death, transformation, and leaving this Earth.

The Dawn Appears with Butterflies (page 35)

This poem too is from my prose poem period that began in the eighties. It was written in the dark before sunrise. I was sitting at an eastern window in the home of a friend in a Hopi village. Her family had come to gather her to go bury her husband in their family cemetery on the mesa. I stayed with the children and their grandmother as they slept. I sat with a pot of coffee and wrote longhand on a pad of yellow lined paper. I wrote out of the grief, including the story of how their daughter had danced the butterfly dance though her father had just passed from this world, because that's how he would have wanted it. Butterflies are great signifiers of transformation.

I just happened to be there, for workshops and performances over in the Tuba City, Arizona, area, so I helped out where I could for the family.

Like many poets beginning, and those of us for whom it is our life, I am excited when I have what appears to be a new poem. For revision I read the poem aloud to myself, then I often read it aloud to someone else, often my husband Owen Sapulpa, or my daughter Rainy Dawn Ortiz. Reading to someone else extends the hearing range. You can hear more exactly what is working in the poem, and what is not serving it. The next level is reading it aloud to an audience. I would not generally suggest it, but it is highly effective! This is where you hear exactly what works and what doesn't—and so does the audience. It's the best proving ground, and possibly the most humiliating!

I read the first version of this poem at my performance in Tuba City a few days later. It was written on three sheets of legal paper. I usually take a draft of a poem from the handwritten page to the computer, or before computers, to a typewriter. I did not have a computer with me and remember revisions on sheets of paper. As I read, I realized excruciatingly, line by line, that it wasn't working.

When I finally took the poem to the computer and revised it many times over, only a few of the original lines remained:

Wings of dusk
Wings of night sky
Wings of dawn
Wings of morning light
It is sunrise now.

Perhaps the World Ends Here (page 38)

I remember starting this poem and following it. As I wrote I felt a wiser-than-me version at the helm of speaking. I did not know where I was going as I wrote, only that I was intrigued and had to follow the words, the music, wherever it was going to go. I revised as I wrote but did not stop the flow of the voice. I love the surprises and turns. They invite me to play. That is the best part.

The voice of my poems is not something I had to search to find. It was there, even before I agreed to write poetry. As I write, this voice has a cadence, a presence, and a need to see where this alchemy of consciousness, wordsmith-ing, and architecture will take us. I say "us" because I am aware of an exchange, a kind of call-and-response between this "voice" and me.

My voice is older, and I am finally growing into it. There were times I abandoned it. It did not go well. The poems are not memorable. Other times I felt it abandoned me, and I didn't write. Other times we both needed a break because something new was in the works. I had to be patient, not something I am known to be.

These older voices don't usually find their place until they are older in earth years, because they don't go along with current fashions and trends of writing and expression. Recently I advised a fine young poet that it could take a while for his poems to be seen or recognized. He has one of those ancient voices that is trying to find its way when the prevailing style is linguistic pyrotechnics that light up dangerous revelations.

A Map to the Next World (page 40)

Every poet has obsessions, as does every human. One of mine is maps and mapping. I believe that what I am doing as I write poetry is mapping the human soul. It is such an immense project that I will not finish it. It has the shape of Jorge Luis Borges's *Book of Sand*. There are emergence places in the map, marked by poems. And there are maps within the map.

This poem is a map I found and wrote for my third granddaughter who was being born. I looked about at the themes governing the time, those that would mark her generation. One of the stories that emerged at that time was of a visit by the Holy Ones to a blind Navajo elder who lived far out on the reservation and lived traditionally. Because she still tended her prayers, much in the way she tended her livestock, they knew their words would find a place to live in her. Such visits were very unusual. This was the first one known to have happened in hundreds of years. She was told that there would be huge earth changes, destruction, and suffering if the people forgot who they were and no longer kept ways that fed their connection to Earth and each other.

This story marked my granddaughter's birth. It is a map within a map.

Emergence (page 43)

My wandering has taken me many places as I construct this map of the soul. This is from another place on the map, Hollywood in Los Angeles. Imagine being dropped from the sky and landing in a studio apartment next door to a very popular drug dealer, just a block north of Hollywood Boulevard on Wilcox. You are living in an apartment building filled with other refugees of the American Dream. Many of them like you who pronounced at one time or the other in their lives, "I will never live in Los Angeles."

I stopped there for a moment in my life, for a month or less, until I fled to Laurel Canyon.

I could feel the prophecies erupting through the unstable earth over which the city expanded. This was the place of hope, angels, and hungry dreams.

This poem was the map point where all those lost converged.

The Path to the Milky Way Leads Through Los Angeles (page 45)

It is said that when we Mvskokvlke leave this earth story, we return to the Milky Way. I wonder about that path we take, how it winds through our human tragedies and comic sidetracks. Crow or Raven is often present at doorways of transformation. Just ask the poet Edgar Allan Poe.

When I conceived the map of my story, Los Angeles did not figure into the equation. I always thought I would find my way to San Francisco, a city marked by the darkest, deepest ocean and sage poets on every street corner, not the technicolor dream machinery of the City of the Angels.

Equinox (page 47)

This is a poem that became a song. One of the rules of songwriting, I was told, is that the title of the song should occur somewhere in the lyrics. That does not happen here. And, if you are a John Coltrane fan or hang out anywhere near jazz, this title will evoke a Coltrane classic.

The poem would not have been written without the equinox configuration of the sun and moon balanced across from each other in spring. At some places in our lives are points of reckoning. We are called to examine our story and how it fits into the familial or collective story field.

My point of view here is sundown. At sunrise we collect light. At sundown we let go that which no longer serves a journey forward.

It's Raining in Honolulu (page 48)

I have found home in other places in the world. Sometimes home is in a poem or a song, like John Coltrane's *A Love Supreme* or Naomi Shihab Nye's poem "Kindness."

I began making my way to the Pacific islands at birth and landed in Honolulu, on one of the most beautiful of the Hawaiian Islands. It is there I learned how the plants called rain, how there are many winds. Those winds I came to know lived above the Ko'olau mountain range. They each have names and places they call home. It is here that I experienced the thoughts and speech of rainbows. Although there is the existence of thinking and being in those elemental realms, we are all bound by history. Settlers with a culture and value-set that tells them that earth is a resource for buying and selling see earth, water, and our beingness differently than those who see, know, and experience the earth as a person, who know that we are earth.

The illegal overthrow of the Hawaiian government by American businessmen is a wrong that needs to be rectified and will be. The earth and water will have a hand in it.

When the World as We Knew It Ended (page 49)

I was in O'ahu the morning the Twin Towers fell, awakened by an abrupt phone ring of urgency. It was my Italian translator and friend telling me to turn on the television. Your country is falling. We were falling. And we fell and fell. We continue to fall. The doves went about their morning calling out, the winds softly wound around the mango tree, rustling the banana tree fronds. They will be left when these stories have run their course. Until then, we make songs and poetry to find our steps along the way, through a rubble of history made by monsters who were once children who only wanted love.

For Calling the Spirit Back from Wandering the Earth in Its Human Feet (page 51)

We get lost sometimes or lose parts of ourselves in our story making. Words got us there. Words can assist in calling us back.

A colleague years back in one of my first academic jobs made a point to tell me, after striding into my office and perching without permission on my desk, that there are two kinds of poets. "Jacob" poets are refined, he reminded me, like Jacob in the Bible. "Are you familiar with the Bible?" he asked. "You," he pointed out, "are an 'Esau' poet." Esau was Jacob's brother who lived far out in the wilderness of the desert. He lacked refinement. He lived like the animals in the wild.

If this colleague's behavior is indicative of civilization, I don't want it.

The so-called "civilized" might argue that poetry is only poetry when it showcases an ability to make complicated, metrical literary constructions in classical verse forms. The act of writing poetry, then, becomes a purely mental, technical game only a few, and only the most highly educated, are capable of playing.

In retrospect, after nearly forty years, I should have responded that I would rather live in the wild with the animals. Poetry is found there. It is without pretense, closer to the singing roots of language.

Ultimately, there is no hierarchy. All poetry has roots in orality. Those who perfect the use of language, whether it be in poetry, lyrics, storytelling, or other forms of oratory, know intimately that words can create and destroy. The better and tighter the craft and care, the finer the trajectory.

I don't recall what I said in that moment, or if I said anything at all. This experience was to be repeated in various versions along the way. My relationship with poetry remains complicated, contradictory, and mysterious. Poetry is as demanding of me as I am of poetry.

Rabbit Is Up to Tricks (page 54)

This poem appeared first in the opening of my one-woman show *Wings of Night Sky, Wings of Morning Light*, performed at the Autry Museum in Los Angeles in 2009. It was written in the manner of a Mvskoke origin story, how I might tell it in contemporary times. It is my invented version. Rabbit, or Cufe, is a trickster figure who rides the edge of ethics. With him, the unimaginable happens and his upsetting actions stir up the community. Because of him we see our humanness with stark clarity and can laugh at ourselves even as we pick up the broken pieces.

When something emerges in the world it has a life span dictated by the origin story, by intent, and by how it plays out in the story field. The consequences of an action may take some time to play out, even lifetimes. Or it may happen in an instant. So it is with creative pieces, with art. What we create is born of a time, a moment, and continues. Some events rocket then diminish. Others play out slowly over millennia. This poem came into fullness during the reign of a falsely elected leader who was a dangerous fool. Perhaps that was the purpose of the poem, something I had no prior knowledge of as I assisted the poem into the world. It found its place in time ten years after it opened the performances of my play.

No (page 56)

I was asked by Sam Hamill to submit a poem for an antiwar anthology of poetry he was editing, *Poets Against the War*, which was published in 2003.

My tendency is to take a longer view, to skirt popular or current fashions of writing poetry. Or should I say, that is what my voice insists on doing, even as I thrill to what is original and fresh.

There have been wars since greed, envy, jealousy, and hatred have existed in humans. I like to believe there will be time and place when this is not so. Deliberately cutting back to uncomplicated syntax allows for sharpness of image and the unspooling of contradiction.

This Morning I Pray for My Enemies (page 58)

This is the second prayer in this collection, although I consider each poem to be a kind of prayer. John Coltrane taught me this with his saxophone. Each poem is a song, lamentation, or praise to Creation. Creation is everywhere within and about us. Which means, because we are in a plane of polarity, that destruction counterbalances. Destruction can be as essential as weeding a garden or erasing a word that isn't working for a line. Or it can be tremendously damaging.

Praise the Rain (page 59)

The rhythm of the rain took over the patterning in the poem. I followed it and found a poem. I am often guided by rhythm. I have learned that my creative impulse is primarily kinetic and visual. This bears out frequently in my poetry.

Speaking Tree (page 60)

This poem emerged from misery. I took my awareness to the trees so that I could hear and speak in another way, from another point of view. When my attention shifted and opened its ears to the nearby trees I became a stranger, a kind of distant species, to the pain cycling through me from love lost. The poem taught me there is always longing. Our desires create the longing. It need not feel like destruction, rather like the sound of winds rattling the leaves of trees.

Fall Song (page 62)

This is a love poem. I remember Leslie Marmon Silko telling me how, when Route 66 used to be the major east–west two-lane highway, it went right by Laguna Pueblo. Once there was a terrible wreck and, in the morning, she went out to survey the damage. What told the story, the aching loss of it, was a small personal item, like a child's teddy bear, or a shoe. So it is with the event of finding love. His jacket hanging next to mine in the hallway told the story. That image is like a song that holds memory, the songs we all listen to again and again to catch lost memories to hold them close to us.

Sunrise (page 63)

I remember being in refuge from some event or the other that disturbed and hurt. It could have been an event of the collective or personal, or both. I woke up that morning to sunrise and went out and stood beneath a cottonwood. A Pueblo friend told me how, before they used eagle feathers, small cottonwood branches with leaves were used to clean the body. That morning I saw how the cottonwoods stood witness. And I appreciated that no matter what happened that day before, or whatever grief steals us in the night, the sun over the horizon brings fresh hope, a pathway to make it through another day.

Break My Heart (page 64)

Elise Paschen asked for a poem for her forthcoming anthology, *The Eloquent Poem: 128 Contemporary Poems and Their Making*. One category was "ars poetica," poems that explain the art of making a poem. "Break My Heart" is about both the making of a poem and the making of a life.

Washing My Mother's Body (page 66)

After my mother took her last breath, let go her earth story for the next part of her journey, I stayed with her body alone. I spoke with her earth body, sang quietly, and decided that I would wash her body. I had never been part of such ritual but felt it was important. The next thing I knew, employees from the funeral home arrived with their noise and gurney. I said no, I want to wash my mother's body. This set up a conflict between those in the family who wanted her body taken out and me, the one wanting to wash my mother's body. Because I didn't want conflict to mar our mother's journey, because death, like birth, is an immense moment of tenderness and vulnerability, I let her go. It wasn't until several years later as I wrote the book of poetry that would become *An American Sunrise* that the poem moved through me, surprised me. I learned that I could wash her body in a poem. I was able to fulfill what I thought was an important part of taking care of the ending of an earth story.

Funny though, the poem wasn't directly in the theme of the collection, but my mother has a way of stepping into whatever story I am writing, whether it be memoir, books of poetry, or music.

How to Write a Poem in a Time of War (page71)

What compelled me most as I wrote this poem was how the phrasing of rhythm took over. Often when I read or perform this poem I feel as if I am improvising on my sax and each phrase is a musical phrase rather than successive lines of poetry, one just beyond the others. This poem is a teacher, like the best poems that I write or read. I had no idea how it would end, and I did not, nor do I usually, write toward a conclusion. I might think I know where it is going but I have learned to be open to the journey, to what the event of writing a poem has to teach me. I learned as I wrote that every war is contained within each war. I did not want to forget the suffering of the Syrian families as bombs rained down on them. I will not forget the father holding twin baby girls who were killed in the fire.

When I got to the end of the poem, I was surprised by what happened. There was a grandfather who saw soldiers with guns come to take the people away to Indian Territory, across the Big River. He did not want the children to forget who they were or where they came from, so he blew into them songs that carried maps that would show the way back, that would remind them who they were. Those songs were made to travel through generations.

Maybe that's what these poems, these songs are doing when we make them. When we speak them, they are given impetus as they find their way. When we sing them, they fly.

Running (page 75)

I did not know at first if this poem belonged in the collection I was working on at the time, *An American Sunrise*, which is concerned with history, with the illegal removal of our Native peoples from the Southeast to Indian Territory, particularly the Monahwee and Carr lines of my family. Yet, I decided that the poem did fit in the overall theme of the book. There is no place to fit the kind of evil that uprooted our people from our homes. Where does it go? We continue to carry the grief through generations until we can untangle it and are able to lay it down. Otherwise, it continues to grow in us, turn against us, and take us down by any means, including self-doubt and self-hatred via addiction of one sort or the other, one generation after another.

Somehow, we make it through, though there are moments when the story could go either way. Poetry, music, and image-making have been my way to turn the hatred back, to let it go, to use the materials of destruction to make beauty.

My Man's Feet (page 77)

This poem is a love poem, even as it is an ode to my husband's feet and a poem outlining the layers of history from first contact with those who arrived from Europe in ships, to atomic power, to the intimate now, as it moves from East to West.

Tobacco Origin Story (page 79)

I have always wanted a place to fit the story my cousin George Coser Jr. told me, a story probably told to him by his father, about the origin of tobacco.

We Mvskoke know the tobacco plant as a helper. We are taught of its power. And like any power when used properly and carefully, it can be a healer. When it is abused then it can be destructive.

Tobacco is a beloved plant, and the story of how it became a killer has everything to do with colonization and the perversion brought by such a process. It is a story motivated by greed. And ultimately the story is not so much about the plant, but how the plant's power was manipulated.

I had begun experimenting with syllabics and had just made a new form for birthday poems in which a poem contains as many syllabic stanzas as the new birthday age. I wrote one for a friend, the poet Marilyn Kallet, who was turning seventy. There were seventy stanzas, the first stanza was one syllable, the last stanza of the poem was seventy syllables.

In this poem I worked with eleven-syllable lines against seven-syllable lines. I like the music of seven against eleven, as do gamblers.

Redbird Love (page 81)

Yet another love poem. Maybe there are too many love poems, however there will be love poems as long as there are two-legged humans, just as there will be breakup poems. I believe that love poems outnumber breakup poems though I have not registered an exact count.

This is a love poem of one redbird for another. Two-legged humans are not the only humans. I grew close to a family of redbirds when we lived in Tennessee, and we watched a love story unwind through generations and witnessed the coming of age of a young female redbird.

At the same time, it is a love poem for my husband, made of the tenderness he has demonstrated to me.

An American Sunrise (page 83)

This poem was written as an experiment with the Golden Shovel form, a form invented by Terrance Hayes, constructed around the poetry of Gwendolyn Brooks. The rules are as follows: take a line from a Gwendolyn Brooks poem you love and use each word in the line (in order) as an end-word in each line in your poem. You may use more than one line, which will make a longer poem (of course). The form has grown to include other poets and their poems. This poem is referencing Gwendolyn Brooks's classic poem "We Real Cool" with an epigraph "The Pool Players./Seven at the Golden Shovel."

I later turned this poem into a song featured in my album of music, *I Pray for My Enemies*, which includes a killer guitar solo by Rich Robinson of The Black Crowes. I am joined in singing by Lisette Garcia, and I play the alto saxophone solo.

Frog in a Dry River (page 84)

For a time, I lived near the ditch that runs along the Rio Grande River in the northwest valley of Albuquerque. I often walked the ditch and sometimes rode my bike. I preferred walking because I saw more, and my contemplation ran deeper. Depending on the season the ditch was either full of water or dry. In the early spring the ditch was cleaned of debris, then the water was released for planting. In the winter the water source was closed, and the ditch dried up. I got to know where a crayfish family lived and was aware of the frogs who lived along the ditch. Sometimes I sat near the frogs and listened as the water ran. The frogs were very attentive to people and their dogs.

I have learned that when it comes to animals and plants, communication happens without words spoken aloud. There can be no communication if your human mind doesn't allow a space for it. Let your human mind be still or become like the water running in the ditch in a continuous quiet rhythm. Then, there you are—

You learn that every animal and plant is different. They have likes and dislikes, just like us. Some have no need to communicate with humans. Others who do communicate with us are probably looked on with disdain by their community.

When I lived in Hawai'i a Brazilian cardinal had a different schedule than all the other birds that I fed with seed every morning. I would sit at my desk, writing, like I am now, a few hours after feeding the birds, and I would feel him nudge me to come out. I would get up, look out, and there he would be, waiting for me to bring him down a small handful of seed as he requested. Sometimes he'd bring one of his children.

Prepare (page 86)

I opened my memoir *Poet Warrior* with this poem. With any collection I include a ritual-like opening, to acknowledge place and time and the keepers of place and time, or to give a blessing.

This piece then went on to close a song "No More Pipeline Blues (On This Land Where We Belong)" written by Larry Long and performed by Waubanewquay, Winona LaDuke, the Day Sisters, Mumu Fresh, Pura Fé, Soni Morena, Jennifer Kreisberg, the Indigo Girls, Bonnie Raitt, and me. It was released in 2021.

The Life of Beauty (page 88)

I was given an assignment by the *New York Times* to write about beauty. Several artists, scientists, designers, and others were also asked, "Why is beauty important to us?" This poem was my response.

I see the poem as honoring femaleness, and as especially honoring those missing and murdered Native women who have been lost to us.

This poem is now a song on my music album *I Pray for My Enemies*. Within the song I thread an original Mvskoke healing song.

How Love Blows Through the Trees (page 90)

We were sequestered for the pandemic in the early months of 2020. I looked out onto the walkway from our apartment window through the gray arms of winter trees. Usually that walkway is full of workers and visitors in the morning hours. It is a bridge between the art district of Tulsa and corporate downtown. It takes you over the railroad tracks to the Oklahoma Jazz Hall of Fame. On the walkway is a circle called the "Center of the Universe," the site of an acoustic anomaly. If you stand there and call out, your voice echoes strangely back, as if you are in an echo chamber. And not far away is a tall sculpture by Allan Houser's son, Bob Haozous, called *Artificial Cloud*. It has a huge metal ring attached. Visitors like to slam it against the body of the sculpture. It rings deep and loud. That morning there was no one on the walkway. There was no traffic. No one calling out, no ring of metal against metal. It was quiet, a quiet I had never heard in the arts district, a place of many restaurants, galleries, and a huge homeless population who camped a few blocks away.

Like everyone else in the world, I wondered about this killer moving about among us. We knew it had begun its destruction; we didn't know when it would end.

I wrote this poem as a song, not as a poem. Maybe there is more room for sentimentality in a song than a poem. I was missing everyone, those who were also quarantined, and those who had left us.

Sometimes people leave song tracks behind them.

Sundown Walks to the Edge of the Story (page 92)

I peruse my journals to see how dreams have played out and to find starters for poems, songs, and stories. I found a dream I had written a year ago about a friend whom I had just texted because I sensed she was distressed. In the dream, she needed to climb down an embankment to get to the road. There was the color red. I was reading the dream when she responded to my text, then we spoke. The story she told me matched the imagery of the dream, scene by scene. I had just written a new poem, based on a musing found on those same few pages that read, "those nights in early love he spoke to me when I was sleeping." I had also begun reading Dunya Mikhail's book *The Iraqi Nights* and thought about storytelling that lasts through generations because it is archetypal and made of mythic elements with a half-life of eternity. The poem too matched my friend's situation.

Somewhere (page 94)
In the year 2021 we as a world community dealt with a pandemic that continues to roam, sicken, and kill. In our Mvskoke community we lost many culture bearers. It was a year of broken communication between peoples divided by false stories and lies, planted specifically to divide the country so it could be taken over by those who wanted the riches of these lands, the labor of these peoples. It was a story marked by racial unrest, set off by the continued divisiveness of white against Black and Native, rich against poor, male against female empowerment, and sparked by the 2020 killing by white police of George Floyd, a Black man in Minnesota.

The year also marked the hundredth anniversary of the burning of Black Wall Street, which had been a thriving section of the Greenwood community in Tulsa, and the massacre of citizens of that community. It is a shameful period of Tulsa history, and a history that was kept mostly silent until this anniversary. We didn't hear about it when I grew up. I spoke with a Black taxi driver on the way to the airport one morning. He told me that they didn't speak of it either in his community because it was dangerous. It could happen again.

Artists of all sorts do what artists are charged to do as artists. We spoke about this history, painted and drew it, performed it, sang it, and wrote poetry, because none of us wanted this disrespect and destruction to happen again, not under our watch.

This poem is my contribution. I didn't know how I would write a poem about massacre and the massacred, about a town and a people destroyed, right here, just down the street, as a result of hatred. As I walked along the street where it happened, I found a story that let me in.

Without (page 97)
We lost many to Covid. My beloved brother-in-law decided, because of false narratives fed to him by pundits online and local religious leaders, that he would not get vaccinated. We argued with him, as did his wife. They were newlyweds, come back together after high school at Indian school. His wife got vaccinated, much to his dismay. Still, she urged him to get vaccinated. He was at high risk. He caught Covid, and this man of much energy and shine was gone suddenly. His loss broke our family heart. We miss him and will always miss him.

I was asked to write a poem for his service. This was the first version. I realized after writing it that it didn't fit him or the occasion. It had a different place to live. I wrote another that particularly fit him and the family.

I wrestled over "hyena" as that animal was not local or Mvskoke. I realized that in that space between living and dying, a space that is narrow and elusive even as it is deep and wide, is the place poetry lives. I travel widely.

ACKNOWLEDGMENTS

❧❧❧

On publication of this collection, it will have been fifty years since my first poems were published in the *Thunderbird*, the University of New Mexico student literary magazine, in 1972. My first poetry mentor was the professor and poet David Johnson. As a student in his creative writing workshops, I learned how to gain technical muscle, how to read and listen far and wide, and how to walk past the gates of mystery with poetry as my key. Gene Frumkin, another UNM professor and poet, also taught me. Like Johnson, and any fine teacher, he challenged me, expected the best, and welcomed me into the local circle of poets. Earliest influences are often the most potent. Leslie Marmon Silko was important to my poetry origin story. I met her when she was living in Ketchikan, Alaska, and had come home to New Mexico for a visit. We began our friendship with letter writing, then she moved home to Laguna Pueblo. She taught a semester at UNM and brought in some major heavy hitters in American literature, including Ishmael Reed—who was at the forefront of the multicultural literature movement, an unofficial initiative to include all American writers in the canon of American literature. Silko taught that storytelling is about making relatives and acknowledging the relationship between earth and sky, between two-legged humans and the rest of human creatures, and between the many kinds of time. Poetry is about singing it.

Throughout these fifty years I have encountered many, many more influences and teachers. You know who you are—I have read your books, listened to your music, admired your performances, your art, your being. Some of you lived years and years ago. Some of you are plants, animals, elements, and places on earth.

What is exciting and profound are those who follow in this path, much as I followed in the path of those who preceded me, like James Welch, Alexander Posey, Meridel LeSueur, and Audre Lorde. You know who you are. You are compelled to walk this poetry path even if you can't explain exactly how or why you must take it on.

For this event of publication, it took the efforts and inspiration of many. First, I want to thank my editorial assistant, Jennifer Foerster. She lent another ear to these poems and selections and helped with all the back and forth with editors and agents and listened to my concerns and comments. Mvto.

Thank you to my editor at W. W. Norton, Jill Bialosky. We've worked together since our first book, *The Woman Who Fell from the Sky*, published in 1994. Here we are. Thank you for your belief in these poems, in the power of poetry to make social and spiritual change. Literature teaches us that this whole world is sacred.

Thank you to the whole staff at W. W. Norton, including Drew Weitman, Jill's assistant who sees to the details. What a celebration we will have when we can all meet in person.

I also wish to acknowledge Anya Backlund at Blue Flower Arts for her support in getting me from here to everywhere, and Jin Auh from the Wylie Agency for her astute assistance in all things literary. And Brenda Pipestem for her ongoing wisdom and advice.

Mvto my beloved Owen, this poet's amused and amusing good-looking muse.

Thank you, my many children. These poems are part of your legacy. You inspire me Ratonia Ray Clayton, Raho Nez Ortiz, Phil Dayn Wilmon Bush, Rainy Dawn Ortiz, Christopherson Chico, Sandra Sapulpa, Farron DeerLeader, Star Sapulpa Allen, Owen Sapulpa

Junior, Marissa April Sapulpa, and all the many grandchildren and great-grandchildren.

It's also important to acknowledge the trees, metals, waters, and various elements that go into such a production that results in books and digital content. Mvto/thank you as you assist the messengers, the singers.

Each of these poems is a gathering place or counterpoint of many landscapes, visions, and histories. Each poem is an altar for remembering, even forgetting.

Finally, every day I miss the elder teachers, writers, and family members who passed on knowledge to me in stories, poetry, and songs in the many various means through which transmission is possible. Though I can no longer touch you, earth to earth, your words, voices, and memory presences remain to guide me with your love.

I offer this in gratitude.

Joy Harjo/Joy Harjo-Sapulpa
Tulsa, Oklahoma/the Muscogee (Creek) Nation Reservation 2022